PORTAL

A LIFETIME OF PARANORMAL EXPERIENCES

ANNA MARIA MANALO

BEYOND THE FRAY

Publishing

BEYOND THE FRAY

Publishing

In memory of my uncle

ACKNOWLEDGMENTS

I thank all my contributors who shared their incredible experiences with me and patiently endured my numerous questions. Without them, there would be no book. Since the first edition, I have kept in touch with some of the experiencers and witnesses, from as far as Southeast Asia to those who live near me in Bucks County.

From overseas, I thank my new friends who continue to watch for other events in the night and have a newfound curiosity. I believe as they believe now in the existence of other dimensions of reality, other forms of beings, and creatures too strange to imagine that roam the earth.

To all of them I thank them for their courage in participating in this fantastic narrative.

Anna Maria Manalo
Bucks County, Pennsylvania
1 May 2021

"We will find that there are planes of existence, other dimensions and other universes existing side by side with this one.
Once we have removed the blinders that impede our progress, we will know that we are only limited by our imaginations."

Dolores Cannon, *The Custodians*

INTRODUCTION

The second edition of this book comes on the heels of a pandemic that wreaked havoc on thousands, if not millions of lives. However, the pandemic is also a natural device, occurring every hundred years on this planet. It is a natural flow of the earth and serves, in this case, to give humanity an opportunity to pause and reflect on things that matter.

For me in my corner of the world, the pandemic proved a time of reflection and an acknowledgement of mortality – and our limited time on this three-dimensional realm. Those limits are imposed upon us, in my opinion, in order that we may understand the true meaning of life, why every being, animal or plant is sacred and how our thoughts have the power to manifest in reality and in action. That three-dimensional time frame in which we are challenged to make critical choices within a lifetime determines the course of our future lifetimes. To me, the idea of karma, of cause and effect, is very real. Indeed, some of the stories here show how violence in war and in individual action (cause) lead to malevolent effects, be it in hauntings and residual terrifying energy (effect). For me and for others who believe in the doctrine of reincarnation, the purpose of one lifetime on this planet is to gain spiritual advancement that hopefully gets us closer step by step to divinity. It is just one lifetime among many.

As in the previous edition, this slim volume contains encounters based on true events. All of the accounts are from witnesses I interviewed firsthand as well as, in some cases, told to me by relatives who lived in close proximity. Some of the events began when I myself was an infant, and in those cases, I relied on stories from family members I trusted. The first encounters comprise the neighborhood I lived in, which at the time was a small hamlet in the outskirts of tropical Manila, now a large metropolis and international hub for travel within the Pacific Rim.

Since most Westerners know little of the culture of the Filipino people, I have introduced the reader in the initial chapters of this book to the background of this post-Spanish colonial country. I think this is essential in order to better appreciate and understand the encounters within the embeddedness of that culture.

The child called "Lisa" and her family constitute several chapters in the first half of this book. Since the encounters were pervasive and extensive, I felt they merited much attention and, in the telling, reveal to the reader the severity of how evil can manifest when humans on the earth do evil things. Evil begets evil. Beings who are of a lower nature – such as demonic entities, spirits who committed murder as people in their lifetimes, as well as other otherworldly beings of a lower nature – are attracted to negativity and violence. They themselves manifest and feed, perpetuate and prolong misfortune, malice and more violent actions on the living.

However, there is also the other end of this duality: The divine, the benevolent and the compassionate. To these beings, we owe our survival, our hope, our health and our joy. It is because of this dualism that the earth in its present state continues to balance, and this balance you experience constitutes the nature of reality.

These forces of good and evil, positive and negative, make up the panoply of creation as intended by a universal energy that man is currently grappling to understand. We, I believe, as the most intelligent creatures to date on this planet, are here to lend credence and live lives that fulfill the ultimate mission of a biodiversity that has been born in balance with these dual forces. However, for us to understand, we must understand what we cannot hear, see nor feel unless our third eyes are open to the infinite – and that openness to a reality beyond our visible world is key to wholeness and discovery.

I present you with the second edition of my book.

I hope you enjoy it in great health and with much abundance.

Anna Maria Manalo
May 1, 2021

PART I

THE ALAMEDA FAMILY

1. WORLD WAR II STORIES

L isa's grandmother Adelaida used to say that if you feel you're being watched, you are. She would sit in the kitchen, dicing vegetables with the ever-present housemaid by her elbow waiting for "Mrs. Alameda" to dole out further instructions. That maid, "Muling", a nickname for a much-longer name given at birth, stuck with her for years. In the early 1960s before civil rights became a household word in the small intimate community of San Juan, Muling joined their household when she was only fifteen. During her brief employ as a maidservant of eight years, she had seen plenty of frightening "beings" that inhabited the old house Lisa's grandparents had built. It was taken down several years ago when the entire family dispersed all over the globe, leaving the grandmother to join her youngest daughter's household two hours south.

Where Muling is now, no one will ever know. She left to get married to some young man she met while strolling in Luneta Park one Sunday. But her memories of the haunted house, I'm sure, remained with her, as they remained with Lisa.

Nestled midway on Lourdes Drive in the small suburb of San Juan thirty miles north of Manila, the wooden house with a concrete slab for a floor remained cool and breezy in the humid summers and cold during the monsoons of July. Jalousie windows opened to the small and private street and on either side of the house, though one wall was built so close to the property wall that one could sometimes hear the neighbor next door and watch their maid flirt with the chauffeur.

The house's two-storied cumbersome rectangular shape was compensated by its perfect location – a first-class neighborhood where the homes belonged to professionals: doctors, like Lisa's grandfather, a pulmonary specialist; architects, like her uncle; businessmen like her youngest uncle and artists like her aunt Sandy; teachers like the oldest daughter, her aunt Sonya; and finally, her mother, Neala, who became a journalist for the *Manila Bulletin*.

Just three miles away was the coveted Saint Paul's, a primary school that had a high school and four-year college all in one campus. It was founded by the sisters of St. Paul de Chartres of France. As a student, it was in that school's halls where students encountered a grave that would not be covered and a floating nun without a face: Her earth-bound spirit roamed the elementary school's chapel.

San Juan had its medley of fiestas: town celebrations in honor of Saint John, its patron; family weddings, lavish and grand; small gatherings made intimate by multiple dishes prepared by the family: Lisa's grandmother, grandfather and aunt. The tradition of the upper classes helping the local poor was steadfast in the culture of the time. Lisa's grandfather had a practice and an affiliation with the veteran's hospital: The latter due to his service in the army during World War II. He gave freely of medicines and administered much-needed vaccinations to the local children whose parents could not afford doctor visits. Anyone who came to the door from the "other" end of the neighborhood was rewarded with food and free checkups.

In the backdrop of post-World War II, San Juan in the '60s was a prosperous town with churches, private schools, theatres, concert venues, and sophisticated restaurants and stores. It attracted European businesses such as car imports from Mercedes-Benz (used as a taxicab), Citroen and Fiat (bought by an educated and thriving upper middle class), and imported goods from Spain. It attracted tourists from as far as Sweden and as close as Japan, a neighbor who rivaled the Philippines for its natural resources and commerce abroad.

Goods from the UK flowed, from chocolates to sweaters, to wine and perfumes such as Lanvin and the house of Givenchy imported from France. In its heyday before the Marcos regime, Manila and its affluent suburbs showed an unprecedented elegance in dress, manner and the education that sent youth to the best and most prestigious universities in Europe and Northern America as early as 1950.

Despite its affluence and the tenets of Spanish influence in landownership and tenancy still a mode, San Juan harbored a very dark past, as did the surrounding area: the death toll from the world war that ended in 1946. Its aftermath left the stench of bodies strewn in the streets, colonial-style homes demolished, and establishments looted. It was evident that the war with Japan had caused enormous and epic devastation. Schools, theatres and any building left standing were used as makeshift hospitals for both civilians and soldiers alike, who came in droves to my grandfather's care: an abattoir of suffering and malaise. Thousands died from massacres, ambushes and relent-less bombing.

Years and many months later, on the brink of emotional and economic recovery, from the ashes of destruction sprang new development. Hastily shed is the terrifying vision of violence and the rape of women and children and the land made red with the blood of the tortured and shot. But the haste to regroup and rebuild what once was a peaceful and beautiful tropical nation now came with an aftereffect: The effect of suffering and violence.

The hauntings of the unquiet began. Their screams beg for a proper burial and recognition of the dammed and forgotten. As Macapagal sat as the new president in the stately presidential palace of Malacanang, Filipinos encountered creatures and the voices of the dead in the loneliest streets and in homes built over the bones of the unblessed.

Both the earth and the sky have their stories. While the earth moved the dead to a portal beyond, the skies opened to evince sightings singular and disquieting. It is part of folklore that every monster that reveals itself has a story and that the heavens will always surprise us. Indeed it has, time and time again.

In the wake of the final days of the fall of Japan to both Filipino and American forces, Lisa's grandfather, Roberto, hands surgically gloved and mouth perpetually masked, administered to the dying in a makeshift MASH unit. Miles away, with instructions to only return when the Japanese had left, her grandmother Adelaida sequestered herself and four children in an abandoned cloister in the remote jungles of upper Luzon. They had traversed and navigated on foot and by "caretella" – a horse-drawn carriage.

On arrival, they discovered a mostly intact colonial stone and cement building, thus finally finding a haven to hide out what would be the final days of the war and rest. The building appeared to be a cloister. Forever a resilient and resourceful woman of thirty-four, Adelaida, who was a dentistry student, married young and had several children – among them, Lisa's mother, Neala – before the age of thirty-two.

As the children, from ages four to twelve, explored the forbidding and abandoned building, night settled quickly.

Adelaida was anxious to settle her brood in comfortably and safely for the night, thus she gave what she could forage in the jungle to the children as dinner. The food consisted mostly of wild fruit, which at the time was in abundance: "santol" – a sour and seeded fruit, mangoes, guavas and a sweet multi-seeded fruit called "atis". Starving and unable to tolerate another day of walking, the children ate fitfully at a wooden table they found among the detritus and sought beds for the night, missing the comforting rituals of home.

In the midst of this lonely, remote and abandoned building, Neala, the second child from the oldest, strode off to seek a room of her own. Neala was always adventurous and daring, unlike her older, shyer sister, Sonya. As she courageously trotted down the dreary halls, she spotted a relatively comfortable room, somehow missed by the chaos and mayhem that usually precipitated a stressed and hasty departure to avoid the advancing Japanese.

Large windows that opened to the jungle revealed nicely made beds, three in a row. The sheets appeared spotless, tucked in and made by meticulous hands. Merrily she launched onto the farthest bed, happy with her find and undaunted that the rest of the family had settled in one large room several rooms away.

Night descended; the cicadas sang as frogs gave out a chorus. In a deep sleep brought on by days of walking, Neala suddenly awakened to the night sounds, which stopped as if by a switch. As her eyes adjusted to the dim light of the stars, she saw what she could only describe as a nun in a black habit approaching her from the other side of the room.

As the nun approached in silence, she noted the specter's feet were missing from under the long habit – it was floating towards her. Its face under the veil was a mask of hate, eyes luminous and red with anger. Neala's throat locked, unable to scream. She sat bolt upright, ready to run. The nun reached her, punched her in the leg, and disappeared into the floor like smoke.

Neala screamed.

Several rooms down the hall, Adelaida bolted from her makeshift bed on the floor, where her body had blocked the door against possible intruders. She mentally eyed the location of the three children and noted the fourth was missing as she ran down the hall to the source of the scream.

As Adelaida entered the room, she spotted Neala sobbing on the last bed, one leg red with a welt. She reached down to soothe the eight-year-old and saw the imprint of a large ring on the child's thigh where the nun had hit her.

For several years, the imprint of that phantom nun's ring remained on Neala's thigh. Until the spring of 1962 when it disappeared.

Encounters such as these where a child, in this instance, not only sees a specter but where the interaction leaves a physical mark terrified Lisa the most. This mark lingered for decades. For years, Adelaida reportedly puzzled over the terrifying encounter.

Did Neala encounter a random ghost, who was a nun caught in the crossfire of the assault of Japan; an unquiet spirit angry at the sudden loss of their life after living in a cloister amid a placid landscape? Or was it a malevolent spirit sent to "hex" her later in life? Or was the encounter a harbinger of what was to happen to the family and to Neala in particular?

The ring left a mark with a symbol. Most Catholic nuns wear rings that have a symbol of a crucifix or a saint or even the Virgin Mary. According to Neala, the ring did not have a symbol of such holy figures. It was nebulous or, at the very least, sinister. Was the nun a fallen angel? A nun who was perhaps forced to betray her faith in exchange for her life, but still lost it in the end? One can only conjecture. With the passage of time and the mayhem of war, obscure and remote locales within the jungles of the Philippines have lost records that could have given a clue to the identity of the nuns and even the order.

Adelaida left the location as soon as she felt safer – to move on to other spots where Filipino or American soldiers and fellow civilians could be found. She had children to feed, shelter and protect, which was more important than a child's random encounter with a tortured soul.

The mark was soon forgotten and covered by a dress or skirt, its significance never explored, as it neither swelled nor became infected – until the day the mark mysteriously and suddenly disappeared.

2. THE HOUSE ON LOURDES DRIVE

L iberation Day found Roberto and Adelaida reunited on the streets of Ermita, a busy borough of Manila. Goods from the PX poured in as people thronged the streets, opening shops and restaurants, which needed fixing, and tradespeople climbed ladders to fix broken windows and doors and clear the aftermath of war. It was 1946.

In December of 1946, the fifth child and first son was born. He was christened Roberto – a junior to his father. They settled the infant and his siblings into the newly built large six-bedroom home, built by an architect of their choice. In the zeitgeist of postwar Manila, Roberto Senior's practice thrived. Loyal patients brought lavish gifts of cakes, pastries, a full suckling pig called "lechon", sides of ham imported from Spain, British chocolates and Belgian cookies. As the new house settled its creaks and groans with new furniture, the house shaped like a coffin remained unblessed; its backyard forever dark with slumbering coconut trees and palms, covering the violence of war.

Yards away, separated by high stone walls on the left, were the Mastriles (pronounced "mass-trill-ye"), another prosperous family, who engaged in imports; and to the right, the Arroyos' garden graced their stucco and red-tiled roofs with a medley of dark and light pink bougainvillea. Across the street, the Capistranos' chauffeur sang his morning baritone as the gates opened to let out the master's car, a businessman in the booming financial district of Makati. Unlike these neighbors' homes, the Alameda house was always dark and appeared foreboding from the street for some unknown reason.

On the street, vendors roamed with local ice cream in the unique flavors of the region: purple yam, cheese corn, mango, "macapuno" – a rich medley of coconut sport and cream, and a green ice cream made from lemongrass – its exquisite and unique taste still lingers in memory. To this, add the cacophony of vendors yelling out names of homemade snacks: "taho" – a hot and sweet concoction adapted from the Chinese, made from dark brown sugar and soft soy cake.

At neighborhood bakeries a showcase of European influence: From Spain came the confection polvorone, made from powdered milk, sugar and in varieties of nut; a butter cream cake in eight layers called "Sans Rival" from France; and a medley of homemade sweets for the late afternoon "*merienda*" before the late dinner at eight.

Inside the Alameda house, two servants faithfully made their daily way out: One to market with a list from Adelaida and one to take the laundry to the back of the house in anticipation of the weekly arrival of "Aling Beatrice", the loyal laundry woman with twelve children. "Aling" was a name given to all women preceding their first name as a sign of respect, akin to the designation of "missus" – or "mister", which is "Mang".

Adelaida always dressed in a tailored pantsuit, hair stylishly coiffed in a bun. She wore pearl earrings, and her wrists were always dotted with L'Air du Temps perfume. No matter the season, she always checked her potted plants, which lined the outer walls and graced the windows. Every day is sunny in San Juan except for the monsoon season, which began in July, pressing trees and the abundant foliage to bow to a tormented sky.

Late one evening before monsoons, as the maid, Muling's predecessor, cleared table scraps from the dining table, she heard the feral cats scream in the backyard. Curious, she carried the scraps, meant for the cats, and exited the kitchen into the dark beyond.

A large backyard with an assortment of fruit trees and palms graced the uneven lawn. The young maid, in her early twenties, undaunted by the dark, strode to the back where the plates for the feral cats lay in wait. As she walked past the laundry area where Aling Beatrice had left large blocks of soap for the week's laundry, she noted that the cats remained standing a distance away. She thought it odd, as the cats, which relied on the table scraps, were always eager at her appearance to approach and start their chorus of hunger.

As she summoned the cats by name, she sensed a presence nearby and started clattering the spoon against the side of the plate, becoming nervous at the likelihood of an intruder. Instead, she heard what she thought was an intake of breath close to her left ear.

The lone spotlight dimmed, but not enough to completely render the area dark. As she turned towards the sound, eyes now luminous with fear, she dropped the plate as she saw what she thought was a man. Hunched down on thin legs, arms crossed against its chest, was a figure that appeared to be a man in tattered rags, gaunt and the color of night. But it wasn't a man. Its eyes were wide, large and red, and it exuded a menacing grin from teeth jagged with dirt. The specter was jet black, but it was more the semblance of a dark shadow with definition.

The maid turned and ran, heedless of the plastic plate and

the scraps of food, which now littered the ground. As she neared the kitchen door, Adelaida emerged, holding another plate of leftovers and a plastic ladle. The fear on the maid's face made Adelaida take a step back as the girl sobbed and recounted what she'd seen minutes before. She adamantly refused to return to the backyard in the dark.

Adelaida strode forward, plate in hand, annoyed at what she believed was the maid's imagination, but as she neared the laundry area, all sounds of the night stopped. She noted that the outdoor light had flickered one last time and died. She paused in her tracks as the cats approached, and put down the plate. As she reached for the outdoor switch, she felt and heard breathing by her ear.

Swiftly, Adelaida turned on her heel and in the corner of her eye saw a bipedal figure in black leap over the ten-foot wall without a sound. Quickly she dashed to the kitchen, locking the door as the maid waited for her to confirm her sighting.

"It's an intruder."

The maid shook her head, terrified.

Lisa's grandmother looked out the window into the night and observed the darkness as the feral cats continued to feed.

"They'll probably eat all the food on the ground you left. No need to clean up. Tomorrow I'll call the police."

The maid nodded, shivered and retired for the night.

"*Salamat* (thank you), Missis."

Adelaida shut the kitchen light off. Behind her, the gaunt man watched from the window. She turned just in time to catch him fade into the night in a wisp of smoke. Then she knew. An involuntary shiver ran up her frame, raising the hairs on her arms.

The next morning Lisa's grandfather Roberto, a pipe perched at the edge of his mouth, listened intently to Adelaida's intruder story while the maids trotted restlessly in the kitchen. A busy man trained in science, he scoffed at the maid's version of the story as superstition and strode off to make ready for his practice.

The police were summoned, and as neighbors eagerly awaited news to find out if there was a burglar in their peaceful neighborhood, no traces were found of the dark and sinister stranger. However, a hint of what was to come revealed itself when the other maid, an older woman, keen to gossip, was meandering outside the house gates one evening. As she stood talking over the week's events with a neighbor's servant, they both turned and spotted a woman in a long dress industriously sweeping the front curb of the Mastrile home. As they watched the woman across the street by the neighbor's front gate, she suddenly disappeared. The two dispersed and ran inside their respective houses, terrified.

Neighborhoods such as these seldom encountered strangers or intruders. Small, ensconced in protective isolation by virtue of people who watched over each other, knew each other, and with the reputation of prominent last names, it was rare for a stranger to enter the area without being noticed.

In Filipino society, where hospitality and generosity is a must, a stranger who walks in or visits a neighborhood, as tourists later do in this particular neighborhood, is usually introduced by whoever invited them. It is usually done informally when neighbors visit, curious as they may be to make contact with the stranger. Tourists, who are usually from Europe, may walk the peaceful streets and are watched from afar. During that time, they were considered a novelty for their appearance, dress and manner – and assumed to be from Spain.

Help is readily offered if someone is lost or especially when an entire family with children are spotted attempting to walk the edge of a busy street – or an intersection where a sidewalk does not exist. Because Filipinos are predominantly Roman Catholic, they adhere to the tenet that the next stranger you may meet and choose to help may be Christ in disguise.

3. ROBERTO SENIOR

As was his custom, Roberto showered upstairs, changed, and grabbed his medicine bag and a clean lab coat from his lab in the rear second story of the house. It is this makeshift home laboratory, later dismantled to make way for a sixth bedroom, that became the most haunted area of the home.

Between wooden shelves that held the trappings of a doctor's wares were several jars, flasks and paraphernalia that bespoke of a man well versed in the art of pharmaceuticals. Back in his day, medical colleges trained their students not only to diagnose and heal, but to be able to concoct simple medicines for colds, coughs and common ills without relying on ready-made medicine. This expertise came in handy on the battlefield, where medicines were scarce, but ingredients might be available.

Among Roberto's potent and effective medicines was a solution called "bromoform" – a tasty, but effective medicine in liquid form, which helped Lisa as a child to surmount coughs, colds and bronchitis. He concocted throat swabs that tasted strongly of eucalyptus and in days rendered sore throats a history, fevers gone by morning.

The effectiveness of Roberto's cures were well received, and word of mouth in the region spread his reputation as an adept lung specialist. He became well respected, if not loved, by both his patients and his colleagues in the medical community. The practice continued to flourish so that after a few years, the young and vigorous Roberto attracted a partner in the practice, which allowed him some free time away to spend with his family. The couple's generosity, reflected in free medical services and the giving of rice (Roberto's younger brother owned hectares of land dedicated to rice fields), added even more to the family's popularity as benefactors.

This lavish lifestyle – which included frequent large parties, catered and uncatered, large sums contributed freely to relatives, plus vacations in first-class resorts in the upper north of the island – led to some unanticipated financial concerns. The situation was made even serious by the entrance of a *"querida"* – a mistress, who was a frequent patient at his practice. Now able to navigate his day partly away from the practice, he spent free moments with his *querida* and procured an apartment for their trysts despite the financial implications.

Roberto's solution-focused mind solved the financial issues quickly with the advent of Adelaida's sixth pregnancy. In the upstairs laboratory where the homemade medicines were concocted, Roberto's growing concern over the unchecked pregnancy and the financial ramifications of a sixth child brewed in his dark mind a potion not far from the Nazi mind across the ocean. In Roberto's futile attempts to maintain his marriage while juggling the demands of his practice and his new mistress, a malignant solution was born.

In the final trimester, a week before Adelaida was due to deliver, Roberto ascended from the laboratory and carried a vial and a needle to Adelaida's bedside, where she lay in slumber for an afternoon siesta.

As he entered their bedroom, Adelaida roused from sleep, finding her spouse sitting poised to administer an injection in her thigh. As Roberto wiped the area with a cotton ball soaked in alcohol, Adelaida dimly inquired what he was administering. He reportedly told her in vague terms that it was a way to ensure a quick and painless delivery.

In less than an hour, Adelaida went into premature labor, and the infant was stillborn. Unable to fathom that a well-respected man of medicine would harm, if not cause the death of a newborn in the family, Adelaida unquestioningly accepted a sedative, which prevented her from seeing the remains of the infant. Exhausted past questioning to determine what had happened to the infant, she slept.

A few weeks passed as Adelaida recovered from her aborted pregnancy, now but a dim and painful memory to her. She had been told the infant was stillborn and the body donated to the hospital to determine why it failed to thrive. Without a means of livelihood, as she'd abandoned dental school, saddled with five growing children and a household to run, Adelaida maintained her reputation and did not dare question the man who created a grand lifestyle for her and her children. Now in his forties, Roberto had progressed to a verbally abusive and intimidating figure whose attention was now sorely divided between his loving children and a new mistress.

One rainy morning, as one of the new servants dusted in the upstairs bedrooms, curious about the laboratory that no one entered but the doctor, the older of the two maids unlocked the door. As she predicted, the room was musty, and the bottles and jars were covered with dust. She proceeded to clean, justified in her desire to clean the home from top to bottom. As she approached the shelves by the window, she came nose to nose with a large jar wherein a specimen with eyes was suspended in formaldehyde. She gasped and accidentally hit a flask with her dusting mop.

As the flask broke, the maid continued to stare riveted to the contents of the jar: a full-formed fetus, legs and arms curled, fingers grasped together as if in prayer.

She ran from the room.

Bags packed, the older servant gave Adelaida short notice, pointing upstairs at what she had seen, but speechless. As Adelaida made her way up to the laboratory, she encountered the younger maid who had in an earlier story seen the specter in the backyard. The older maid had the shards of the flask and blocked Adelaida from entering. Her face, drawn, pale and in disbelief, told Adelaida everything. Finally, admonished, she moved away. Adelaida entered the room, saw the jar and its contents – and fainted.

Nightfall found Adelaida reclined on her settee in the parlor, the remaining young maid ministering to her, still shaking from the earlier event. When she found Roberto reading in the family room, Adelaida confronted him, and he indicated the offensive jar had been removed and the older maid dismissed without references for trespassing. Roberto explained away the specimen as none other than a dead animal that he had found in the backyard.

That evening, Adelaida's older servant called from her sister's house in the province to tell her the house was now cursed with murder. The older woman pressed her that the infant must be given a Christian burial to lessen the malevolence that could follow. Adelaida, fearful of what the woman's knowledge could bring, offered her a sum to silence her "superstition" and explained that the object in the jar was a dead animal, as her husband had explained.

The young servant went about her business, avoiding the lab and the backyard from her previous encounter. Upset over her miscarried child, Adelaida spent time with her half-sister and cousins, who now knew all was not well in the doctor's household. The children grew as the couple's marriage continued to falter in an aura of distrust.

Two years later, the youngest child was born despite the doctor's desire: A boy. Little did Adelaida know that this birth, welcomed by Roberto, was allowed to go full term because the infant was male. He already had four girls. A second boy was perfect. He would be a companion and playmate to Roberto Jr., who was now four years old.

Soon after the sixth child's birth, the other jars disappeared from the lab, and Roberto started clearing the lab for a sixth bedroom. As the new infant was moved next to Adelaida's bedside, Roberto moved out of the house and gave his son Roberto Jr. the former lab as his new bedroom as a parting gift. With his oldest daughter now employed as a teacher, he had in effect relinquished his financial responsibilities to her and the education of the two sons to his wife. He moved in with the mistress, who had started her own family with him.

Several years would transpire before the next tragedy would occur. However, the stage was set for a curse to take place in a home that saw suffering in war and suffering in peacetime. The house was now a virtual portal for evil to enter. In a few more years, as Roberto's younger daughters bloomed to become beautiful young women, a third crime would occur that forever sealed the fate of the family.

Meanwhile, a new anomaly at Lourdes Drive would reveal itself.

4. THE UNBORN

L ate one evening, with Adelaida's oldest daughter, Sonya, teaching evening classes and two of the three younger girls out on the town with friends, Adelaida and her sons had just finished their evening meal. The third daughter, Melissa, was alone upstairs, packing to visit with her uncle Celso, who grew fond of her.

Born with a congenital defect that left her with short legs, Melissa could no longer tolerate the belittling she suffered at the hands of her preteen brothers, who called her "*pato*" (duck) owing to her waddled walk. She would leave in tears and would only return as an adult to take care of her first niece, whom she later came to dote upon, as did the rest of the family. That was Lisa.

Dr. Alameda's one and only younger brother, a bachelor, lived alone in the family's large ancestral home built in the 1830s, where he and his older brother grew up. As a landowner and businessman, Celso ran a rice plantation of eighty hectares in the rural region of Pagsanjan, a tourist town known for its famed waterfall. In this pastoral setting, Melissa blossomed into a young woman who lived amicably and peaceably with neighbors who grew fond of her ability to sew.

As Melissa packed her clothes for what would become a lifetime stay, she emerged one last time to say goodbye to the cats she so loved and cuddled. In the backyard where the animals slept, Melissa discovered a den of kittens. As she stooped down to pet them, fondly naming a striped black tiger "Bridget", she sensed someone watching her. As she unfolded her short legs, she nudged a foot encased in flip-flops. Hairs on the back of her head rose as her ears hummed. Quickly, she took in the sandaled foot, which she recognized was neither one of her brothers'.

She looked up in surprise at the sudden intrusion. Above her, the gaunt man with red eyes glared back with evil. It was the man the younger maid had seen several months ago. The servants had finally given the specter a name, "Mumbo Jumbo", to give the encounters some levity.

Seeking to grab hold of a nearby chair where the kittens nestled underneath, Melissa fearfully sought to stand, stumbling, finally running back to the house. As she neared the entrance to the house, she saw what she thought was a small child standing alone in the middle of the driveway. Except its eyes were completely a dull black.

As Melissa entered the door, she slammed it shut and encountered her brothers chuckling at the far side of the dining room. She climbed to the window to check the whereabouts of the "child" in time to catch something black scurrying in the direction of the backyard.

This time, no police were summoned.

Returning distraught to her room upstairs, bags packed and ready, Melissa sought the solace of her small room. She reached to shut the window above her alcove bed in trepidation, afraid of what she might see. This window was directly a floor above where she'd encountered the specter of the man. Successfully, she pulled it shut in relief. She made her way off the bed and to the bathroom across the hall near her mother's bedroom.

Unable to reach the bathroom sink without a stool to stand on, Melissa reached for the homemade stool fashioned by a doting uncle under the sink. As she clambered up, now able to reach the faucet, a breeze wafted in from the small window to her right.

She glanced out and fell off the stool from fright.

Outside the window, peering in, was a child floating with no eyes. Its mouth, partially open, revealed small jagged teeth. A "*tiyanak*" was the later explanation. A *tiyanak* is a kind of vampire in Philippine mythology.

Downstairs, Adelaida heard a thud from the kitchen, where she and a new maid were clearing the dishes from dinner. She rushed upstairs to check on Melissa, whom she found sobbing on the floor, a large bump on her thigh from when she fell from the stool.

Adelaida checked the window where minutes ago Melissa had seen the specter. She insisted on what she had seen and corroborated the maid's encounter with the male ghost.

There was nothing there but a slight breeze from the quiet night.

The next morning, Melissa left with Celso's chauffeur, not to return to San Juan until that fateful morning of 1962.

5. THE HORROR OF LITTLE BAGUIO

I n the summer of 1959, Neala, now a captivating young coed, married her college sweetheart, Ernest. The couple, both bent on careers in writing, settled in the small hamlet of Little Baguio to start a family. They chose to rent in a newly built townhouse complex perched at the edge of a creek. Neala had a degree in journalism and so did Ernest, but he sought a career as a freelance writer and to begin by getting his sheaf of poetry published. Both sides of the family disagreed with the marriage, as Ernest was a sensitive young man who had suffered bouts of depression, and Neala, his total opposite, was strong-willed, outspoken and wanted her way even as a young child.

Neala's episode with the nun in a black veil, which left the mark of a ring on her thigh, was long forgotten. It was to be a new life for the young couple, just shy of a few months after college graduation. Young and idealistic, the new marriage was still in its first months when Neala learned she was with child.

The complex's first tenants were new families on both sides of Neala and Ernest's townhouse. As with the others, their unit was large, with a living room and TV room area spanning the entire front facing the common driveway – and the back was the kitchen and dining room. A large window, which spanned the kitchen and dining rooms in the back, gave a view of the trees lining the creek just yards away. Sunlight filtered in through the trees and into the kitchen and dining area during the day. A view of the creek showed residences across the water, which flowed clean and clear. The window was almost as high as the ceiling and as wide as the size of the wall. The large windows were the same size on the second floor, which spanned the breadth of the three bedrooms, which sat side by side at the back of the townhouse. The proximity and size of these massive windows let in air and sunlight and will be important to remember later on.

Between the kitchen and dining area was a staircase underneath which the live-in maid slept. The stairs led up to the three bedrooms and a bath and closet opposite the hall. The center bedroom was the new nursery, right at the top of the stairs. To the right of the stairs was the first bedroom, which was used as Ernest's study, where he did his writing, and to the left was the master bedroom across from the main bath.

In the early 1960s it was common for grown female children to live in or near their parents' home until they married. Little Baguio was a mere three to four blocks from Adelaida's house. So convenient was the living arrangement that despite a live-in maid, Neala still sought to arrange to have food delivered to the townhouse from her mother's house in San Juan. Still lovingly prepared by Adelaida, dinner came with fresh rice, three main courses, and the requisite medley of desserts now prepared by older sister Sonya, who was a home economics teacher at a local high school situated an hour away.

Neala spent most of her days with her infant, shopping with her friends, and visiting with her sisters. However, this idyllic lifestyle was not to last: as the year drew to a close, the schism between Ernest and Neala became more pronounced: from child-rearing to finances, to time divided between in-laws. As Ernest's parents continued to lavish support for his writing and encourage him to visit an older brother's thriving bookstore, Ernest sank deeper into a depression. It was a depression made deeper by a force that appeared in the midst of the couple's growing discontent with each other.

In the early evening twilight, Ernest started reporting a creature that he claimed "wanted to take his soul". It would manifest itself at the large window that spanned the breadth of the three bedrooms upstairs, once the sun began to set.

In the crib next door, Lisa, just an infant at the time, was reportedly sensitive to the appearance of the creature, crying and screaming to herald its appearance. The nursery window connected to the window just next door – Ernest's office and den. The maid would anxiously check the infant's welfare and would dash upstairs. But as soon as she appeared at the door, the being would disappear – or so it was reported.

Neala, forever skeptical due to Ernest's history of depression, dismissed his growing fears. Ernest grew despondent, and as the nights progressed and the months moved to the rainy season, she found that he rarely slept. Neala addressed her concerns with her in-laws, and Ernest's father, a bank executive, stepped in.

In the '60s, the advent of psychiatry came to the Philippines in the form of talk therapy, antidepressants and shock therapy. The mode of treatment at that time was invariably electroshock therapy, as medication was still novel and in development. Despite the psychiatrist and psychologist's "talk" to dissuade Ernest of his self-reports of this "creature", Ernest persisted in his accounts of the creature's visits.

The specialists, unable to relate to the paranormal nature of the case as they were trained in the manner of science, dismissed it as hallucination, and the electroshock therapy began. Furthermore, they could not find anyone to corroborate Ernest's sightings except his infant daughter, Lisa, whom he reported exuded terror at the creature's manifestation at the window.

Back at the town home, the creature's continued presence almost every twilight consumed Ernest's waking hours. His apprehensions of being "taken" by the creature, body and soul, started to show in his poetry. His poems, which were an outlet for his internal turmoil, turned even darker, drearier and foreboding. His siblings, who read his opus, became concerned and, from concern, became alarmed when he wrote one poem that began with "The bird that flies is false". Themes of death became prominent.

Ernest had a total of ten siblings, of which he was in the middle. Among them were two sisters who approached Neala to intervene, as well as a brother who was close to Ernest as children and a younger brother who had looked up to him.

As Ernest's brothers and sisters attempted to seek evidence of the creature's existence, Neala responded by reluctantly reaching out to her mother. Unsure of what to do, Adelaida contacted Roberto, the doctor in the family, who had abandoned Adelaida and their growing children years before.

Neala's sense of betrayal by her father became complete: Roberto refused to intervene in the small family's growing problems and referred Ernest's issues back to his own parents. The rift between father and daughter would soon reveal itself again when Neala rejoined her family in the San Juan home a year later.

It was not long before the infant's cries, which heralded the creature's appearance, would save Ernest and win his credibility. One evening, as dinner was being prepared in the kitchen, Lisa, now a toddler, began her earnest screams of terror. Again, her cries brought the maid running up the stairs. But this time, she would reach Lisa in her crib in time to see the visitor outside the window.

Embracing the window, with a wingspan of more than six feet from tip to tip, was a bat taller than a man. Its leathery wings ended in a talon-like grasp at the edges of the window. Its yellow eyes were like a cow's, the semblance of horns protruded from its black head, and it had a goatee at the end of its pointed chin. The face of a goat with the eyes of a cow and a leathery body framed by the wings of a bat. The creature was glaring down at the toddler, who was poised to leap from the crib in abject terror.

The maid, spellbound by the eyes at the window, reached for the baby as she reached out to her with her tiny hands. Holding the terrified child, the maid bolted out of the nursery, sobbing in horror. The young maid's wails brought Neala to the room, and for the first time, she beheld the massive being at the window. Neala described it as the devil himself. Emboldened to protect her baby and subdue the malevolence at the window, Neala reached for a large cross on an adjacent wall and dashed to the window with the cross in both hands. The being "folded" and shrank away from the window. It seemed, according to Neala, to cover its terrifying face with one wing as it drifted down and disappeared. Throughout the entire event, frogs, cicadas and the sounds of the night had completely silenced, only to be replaced by a "humming" sound.

As soon as the being disappeared, the sounds returned. Neala dashed outside and to the creek outside the window. There was nothing there. Sounds of rushing water and the chorus of frogs greeted her. The tree where Ernest reported the creature would appear stood silent and foreboding. There was no trace of animal prints or bat dung.

6. **A DEATH IN THE FAMILY**

B ack in San Juan, Adelaida did not know how to address the terrifying events that seem to be escalating in the town home in Little Baguio. A devout Roman Catholic, she sought relief in the church and always hoped for an answer to every prayer request. She knew from her other children and the servant who delivered the prepared meals that Neala was on her way to tell her the events of the night before. Already convinced there was some type of paranormal infestation in the little home based on her own experiences, she believed it was only a matter of time before the hauntings progressed – and she did not know what to do.

Adelaida knew her daughter was not a staunch Catholic, so when talk of the monstrosity at Little Baguio had reached her, she had concerns about whether prayer and blessings would work, as Neala had a rebellious streak and did not welcome any input from her own mother. However, she was concerned for her first grandchild, a toddler who was now helpless to escape what Adelaida saw as an environment with a malevolent presence.

Neala might rebuff Adelaida's efforts to bring a priest to the home to perform a cleansing rite. Among the siblings, Neala rarely attended mass with the family, unlike the younger sisters, who joined their mother at the local church every Sunday. In light of the past several months, Adelaida knew she had some persuading to do and might need the help of others. An optimist by nature, Adelaida, however, took a step back and saw the unfolding events as a possible way to get her daughter back to the church.

To Adelaida's surprise, Neala appeared, though it was minutes after the mass began. Adelaida hailed a taxi, and Neala willingly accompanied her mother to the church just minutes away. There, Adelaida hoped the priest would have a solution, now that her daughter appeared receptive to intervention. It was a private matter with some urgency, and she knew the respected parish priest would honor confidentiality, sensitive to their prominence in the community. Melissa, who was fortunately home for a visit, stayed to babysit Lisa.

Meanwhile, alone in the house with Ernesto, the maid sat alone in the kitchen, cleaning after the breakfast meal. She glanced up at the ceiling above her with trepidation. Charged with staying in the house to watch Ernest and report anything unusual, the maid was ready to tender her resignation despite the financial needs of her own family in the far-off province of Leyte. Terrified of the being she'd encountered at the window the night before, she clutched a rosary and avoided looking out the window. She decided that if Neala didn't return by nightfall, she would call her sister and persuade her to keep her company until her return, or even perhaps step out briefly for some dinner. What could possibly happen in the few hours while she ate at a local restaurant nearby?

At the church, the parish priest eyed the two beautiful women. Their features betrayed their Spanish blood of Castilian origin, which made them stand out both in appearance and height from the rest of the congregation. He led them into the rectory as soon as the last parishioner had exited the vestibule, sensing the urgency of their visit. He recalled having met Neala once before when he'd conducted the wedding ceremony, but not since then.

He offered his condolences, then his intervention. "I can come to bless the house."

"When can you do it, Father?"

"Next week?"

Adelaida glanced at her daughter with trepidation.

"It's Friday. We don't know if it can wait the weekend."

The priest frowned and looked at his appointment book. "I have a few weddings this weekend. Monday?"

Neala stepped in. "Is that ALL you can do?!"

Taken aback by her vehemence, the priest turned to Adelaida for support.

Adelaida signaled her daughter to calm down and reluctantly agreed to wait the two days. She turned to her daughter as the priest left.

"Let's pray and light a candle on the way out."

Neala whispered en route to the side altar, "Mama, I will make sure he's not alone over the weekend."

"Daughter, make SURE neither he nor the baby are alone."

"The maid is at home with him, and the baby is with Melissa. I need to get out and shop."

As the day grew old, the maid grew weary of her vigil. She reached for the phone in its cradle and called her sister. Upstairs, Ernest typed on his Smith Corona, venting page after page of a sordid composition of the being at the window, an oppressor that became an obsession.

He was nodding off, exhausted, but unable to allow himself to sleep, but the medication the most recent physician gave him would not allow him to sit. Finally giving in, he stood and retired to the master bedroom at the other end of the hall, passing the main bath on the way. He drew the curtains, closing off the only light in the room. His action, a feeble attempt at shutting out whatever might show at the window should he awaken at sundown.

A few blocks away, Neala, eager to get out of the dreary townhouse and the foreboding atmosphere, decided to take advantage of Melissa being able to babysit during her visit. She departed the Lourdes Drive house in the company of older sister Sonya to shop downtown. Stores and boutiques in Manila and the suburbs were usually open late, sometimes until 10 p.m. It was also not unusual for people to dine as late as 9 p.m. At San Juan, Adelaida went about her daily business of running the large household and preparing for the weekend. It was an active household, as the younger children, boys now in their teens, brought friends to the house frequently, so Adelaida was policing their activities as the week drew to a close.

Night approached. A few hours ago, the maid had ventured out of the townhouse to meet her sister at the bus stop to see a film downtown and dinner. It was, after all, calm and uneventful. At approximately eight o'clock, Neala and her oldest sister, Sonya, now heavy with shopping bags, returned to San Juan. They were ready and eager to have dinner with their mother and siblings as well as to check on Lisa, her infant daughter. The weekend had begun, and they were ready to attend some parties and had purchased some new dresses, the latest in fashion. After the shopping bags were divided up, the two sisters separated, Neala to pick up Ernest with the chauffeur so he could join them for dinner at her mother's house. The rest settled down in the parlor to catch up on the day's events with their mother and siblings while dinner was being prepared.

A few blocks away at Little Baguio, the lonely and dark townhouse had one sole occupant. Ernest awakened to a humming sound and a sense of menace. Growing fearful of being alone in the evening, he shot up from the bed and made for the hallway, yelling out the maid's name.

Ernest walked down the steps, turning the lights on in the kitchen and living room. Years later, his siblings and those who had visited always remarked how every room in the house was always lit, which told them he was home. Tonight was no exception. As he walked, he pulled the curtains together to shield his sight from whatever could be at the window. Despondent, anxious and without appetite, he turned on the upstairs hall light and proceeded back up the steps in trepidation. Outside the baby's room, he paused and then entered to pull the curtains together. The hum had intensified, obliterating all other noises of the night.

He reentered his office. As he reached to close the window curtains, the tree outside the window seemed to come to life. His eyes opened wide as he backed away from the window. The humming increased.

Neala's watch on her slim wrist showed 8:30 p.m. The car slowed as she reached for her purse and to open the passenger rear door. The chauffeur sped away after leaving the shopping bags at the open gate of the compound. Neala made her way into the townhouse's front door, knocked, and frowned when no one opened.

She unlocked the door with her key and sensed a complete feeling of isolation and menace. As she surveyed the dark living room, she realized to her consternation that the maid had not heeded her direction to remain home while she was out. Neala switched the lights on, feeling a drop in temperature as she entered the home.

Up the stairs, Neala started yelling Ernest's name. No reply. As she ascended, the temperature, which would normally go up a few degrees on the second floor, plummeted even lower. She shivered with apprehension, having been raised in a haunted house. Since there was no air conditioning in the house, the chill in the air was unusual.

In the corner of her eye she spotted a foot within the open door of the bathroom. She stopped in her tracks and screamed. The maid had just returned and looked over Neala's shoulder to see the abattoir in the bathroom. She turned and bolted from the hall.

R oberto Junior poked his head out the second-floor window of the San Juan house upon seeing Neala's maid, white with fright, running down the street. He was by the window overlooking the street, perusing Katzenjammer Kids comic books he had stashed in his father's army trunk, planning on a late, but quiet Friday night of fun reading after dinner. The teen sensed something very wrong as he saw her running and yelled, "Mama," for Adelaida, who was downstairs in the family room, waiting for the rest to sit down to dinner. Adelaida was watching a film after Melissa joined her, having placed the sleeping infant in the crib nearby.

Adelaida's youngest son, Jose, still up, met up with the maid, who was inconsolable and appeared terrified. Anxious to make out the facts amidst the maid's hysterical babbling, Adelaida sent Jose to run on foot to the home in Little Baguio as Roberto went to call his father. Adelaida was glad she had sent Neala home alone, after both the maid and Ernest failed to answer the phone. She had a sinking feeling it was not the best time to send an infant home with her mother to a house that was infested.

Gifted with a sense of precognition, Adelaida knew in the

depth of her heart that they needed a medical doctor, even if it meant fetching her estranged husband. It was to be one of the most traumatic events in Neala's life. Inexplicably, the mark from the nun's ring had disappeared from Neala's thigh.

Dr. Alameda arrived shortly at the town home, meeting with an ambulance crew, who took Ernest from the home after Roberto pronounced his son-in-law dead. His sons, Jose and Roberto "Bobby" Jr., touched Ernest in disbelief, finding him already in rigor mortis. Ernest had given in to the malevolence at the window, freeing his spirit from torment by slashing his wrists.

The parish priest, the same one whom the women met with earlier, told it was a suicide, refused to have Ernest's body viewed at the church or give him a Christian burial. Despite both families' requests, the priest would not give in. Inconsolable and guilt-ridden for leaving Ernest alone, the maid left of her own accord, fearful of the being that led to Ernest's death. Weeks later, Neala returned to the townhouse with her siblings to clear the home of their belongings. Ernest's parents and siblings took possession of his rocking chair in his office, his Smith Corona and his desk and chair. The furniture would forever remain in his parents' home even after they passed. He was twenty-four years old.

On the morning of the funeral, the family left Melissa in charge of the baby again and prepared to meet with Ernest's family for the mass and burial. Amidst all the preparations while at the San Juan home, Lisa sat alone at the nursery chair and table, eating breakfast. Roberto "Bobby", now dressed in a dark blue suit and tie for the funeral, walked into the nursery to check on little Lisa as Melissa was busy with chores in the kitchen.

He entered, dapper and pressed, smiling at the child.

"Daddy!"

Taken aback, Bobby paused to survey the room.

"You're NOT Daddy!"

Bobby softened, leaning on one knee to soothe the child. "No, it's me, Lisa."

"Daddy was here."

"Oh?"

"Yes, he was sitting right there!" Lisa chuckled happily, pointing to a corner of the room. "He was waving bye-bye."

The hair on Bobby's covered arms rose. He grabbed the child and carried her out to the drawing room.

Dressed in black with a long veil, Adelaida approached the child in Bobby's arms, taking her.

"That's your uncle Bobby, Lisa. Your daddy's not here."

Lisa smiled. "Daddy was in the room. He smiled and waved bye-bye."

"How did you know it was your daddy?"

The child pointed to Bobby's clothes. "He was dressed like him."

Adelaida and Bobby joined the procession to the altar, the casket open for viewing. After weeks of meetings, the family's church in Sampaloc allowed the wake on behalf of Ernest's parents. Adelaida could not bring herself to tell her daughter, Neala, what Lisa, now a babbling toddler, had told her that morning. As she approached the open casket, Ernest lay in a dark blue suit and tie – almost identical to the suit Bobby was wearing. Everyone knew that no one had dared bring Lisa to the wake or give the child an opportunity to see her father in death, dressed in a suit.

Prior to her father's death, Lisa had never had occasion to see ANYONE dressed in a suit. Ernest always wore short-sleeve polo shirts and light-colored slacks, even on weekends. None of his siblings nor Bobby dressed in suits because of the stifling tropical humidity.

A month after Ernest's untimely death, Neala permanently moved with her daughter back to her parents' home in San Juan. There, the family doted on the first grandchild, now orphaned without a father. They created a nursery for her, where she would sleep and play.

Lisa's nursery at San Juan overlooked the narrow, but deep backyard, where in a previous chapter a young maid had seen the "Mumbo Jumbo" – the man in tattered rags with red malevolent eyes. The yard held fruit trees such as coconut, date palm, banana and star fruit. The coconut trees soared high, way over the walls of the homes on either side of the Alameda property, and afforded shade in the heat of the day. The toddler's nursery, the crib now replaced by a large bed, contained a child's armoire, two small chairs and a table to match, and bookcases on two walls filled with toys.

The bedroom had large windows on two sides: One facing the backyard, as mentioned, and the other facing the open laundry area, where Aling Beatrice, now older, had given her laundry maid job to her younger sister, Aling Tale. Between these windows, the child's bed was pushed against them to prevent her from falling in the night. The arrangement allowed the growing little girl to climb up onto the deep window seats on either window. Lisa's other bizarre encounters as a small child would occur in this room.

Right above the nursery, adjacent to Bobby's room, which had been the doctor's laboratory, was the second-floor bath and then a small bedroom where Melissa used to sleep. Although the bathrooms had a small window to afford privacy, this small bedroom had a large window where the edge of the roof could be seen. Into this room, Adelaida had moved after Roberto had made his permanent departure, leaving the master bedroom at the other side of the house for two of her daughters: the oldest, Sonya, and the youngest girl, Sandy, to share.

Houses in the early '50s in San Juan usually had roofs that extended several feet past the windows, where large gutters lined the edges. Due to monsoon rains, which punctuated the country from July to December, roofs were built to shield the upstairs windows from the onslaught of wind and driving rain. The windows had rolling horizontal shutters, but in storms, water can still leach through.

Weeks after Ernest's death, the house had settled back into a routine. Despite the funereal atmosphere that accompanied the tragic death, visits from family friends, extended family and neighbors continued. Condolences and gifts were given, food delivered, and services offered to Neala and her grieving mother and siblings. Family who lived hours away came to pay their respects, as the monsoon season was imminent, and travel would involve flooded roads.

Neala's relationship with her in-laws was strained in a blame-seeking atmosphere that forever affected Lisa's relationship with her paternal aunts, uncles and cousins. No offer to financially assist Neala in her loss was given, and the guilt left an indelible, if not traumatic mark on her psyche, which she carried to her old age.

As Adelaida sought to find a semblance of joy and the normality of routine for her first grandchild, Neala used her degree and talents to seek the career she had placed on hold before Ernest's death. In the backdrop of 1960s Manila, Neala created a career she immensely enjoyed, surrounded by the society of journalists and advertising agencies who coveted her. The career became a haven for her loss and a panacea for what still haunted the San Juan house and the death of Ernest.

Neala entered and "arrived" as a sought-after young journalist who graced the Sunday society pages with her articles, which were matched with top-notch photographers. She was creative, brilliant, outspoken and beautiful. Envied by many women who could not reach the pinnacle at such a tender age of twenty-six, Neala had a line of suitors who were successful in their own right, from photographers, artists, film directors and fellow journalists.

Politically outspoken, Neala would later rebel, as she had as a child against her father, against the dictatorial government that followed Macapagal's democracy: Marcos and Imelda. Later, against the backdrop of a politically unstable government, Neala's discontent with her in-laws and discord with her remaining parent catalyzed her permanent asylum into a foreign country – a country in the '70s that was unprepared, if not intimidated, by her talent and skills.

At the San Juan home, aunts and uncles lavished affection on Neala's child, who was pitied. She was the first grandchild and niece in the Alameda family. Gifts from doting aunts and uncles on Ernest's side of the family also poured in and almost spoiled Lisa, who shied away from attention and sought the refuge of books and animals. Without the benefit of other children her age and an innate desire for solitude, Lisa preferred the company of animals and nature, hiding in the backyard during the day in the shade of the palm tree, reading her storybooks.

When Lisa turned four, her mother's colleagues propelled her doe-eyed wholesome innocence into magazine covers and Rustan's department store ads to pose for clothes of the season, sometimes with her mother. Lisa's faraway look in photographs betrayed the soul who had seen things not of this world and exuded an anxiety of things to come.

One Saturday evening, with everyone gone, the house was silent. Lisa was in the drawing room with Melissa, who had stayed indefinitely as a permanent sitter. Adelaida was upstairs, mending a torn dress while the maid was off. Around 10 p.m., as it was a weekend night, Melissa allowed the sleepy child to stay up to watch *Million Dollar Movie*, which was airing a Shirley Temple film.

As aunt and niece ensconced themselves watching the film, Adelaida upstairs continued to sew. Suddenly, she felt a steady vibration, which she could feel in her chest. She looked up from her sewing at the open window as the cool breeze became noticeably warmer. The vibration became more pronounced.

Something bright like a sudden sun broke through and was shining on the roof. Its flash lighted up the Arroyo family home past the wall, momentarily showing the trees surrounding their roof. The cats, frantic, screamed and scattered below. Adelaida bolted to the window and looked below in time to see the cats scrambling for cover. She thought the flash was lightning, but the light above her continued in searing brightness.

Active and agile in her forties, Adelaida climbed onto the deep casement window, seeking to spot the source of the light over the roof. She shielded her eyes from the glare, but could not determine the source of the brightness, as much as she strained to see.

Then, minutes later, as suddenly as it came, the light cut out.

Adelaida saw stars before her eyes, blinded by the brightness of the aftereffect. Dizzy, she stepped down to the bed and sat down. An overwhelming desire to sleep overtook Adelaida, and she folded and put away her sewing. She lay down on the bed and quickly went to sleep.

Below her, Melissa escorted the sleeping child to the nursery, wary of the window that opened to the dark backyard. She quickly placed Lisa and arranged pillows around her sleeping form and sat on a lounger nearby to do some knitting. She dozed off, unaware of the light above the house.

With morning came the scent of honeysuckle and a rising sun through the window of the nursery. Melissa awoke surprised she had slept through the night in the child's room. Lisa sat, smiling at her from the bed, pointing to the windowsill facing the backyard.

Melissa approached the child, who continued to chuckle as she changed out of her bedclothes.

"What is it? What are you looking at?""

Lisa replied, "Look." She continued to point at the window.

Melissa turned and saw nothing.

She looked back questioningly at Lisa.

"Detlin and Desmond."

Melissa looked and approached the window, perplexed.

Lisa offered: "They left. They're getting more plates."

In trepidation, Melissa grabbed the child's hand and pulled her hurriedly out of the room.

"Wait, they're coming back!"

Lisa turned and kept pointing at the window in frustration.

The door shut.

As Melissa approached the kitchen to tell her mother of the child's babblings, she noted her mother had a tan. Adelaida looked haggard, as if she had not slept.

"Are you all right, Mama?"

"No, I was dizzy all morning."

"You have sunburn all over your face!"

"It stings, Melissa. The moon was so bright over the roof of the house last night. Didn't you see it?"

When Sonya came down to breakfast, Adelaida was ill and nauseous. She hailed a cab and took her mother to her father's hospital, where doctors told them that Adelaida had first-degree burns and a mild case of radiation poisoning. Adelaida recounted her bizarre night with the intense light over the roof.

The doctor explained it away as a sunburn from the day before and enquired if she had been out gardening in the noonday sun. There was no noonday sun, as the monsoon season was around the corner, and the days were increasingly cloudy. Adelaida had not ventured out to tend to her plants in weeks, as the rain was ample. For the next few nights, both Bobby and Jose would sit in the side yard, waiting for the bright "moon" that burned their mother to return.

As Melissa tended to the home during her mother's absence, she dared not tell anyone of Lisa's encounter with something at the window the morning after her mother's sighting. There were already too many events recently that stressed the household. Always the brunt of jokes, she did not want to add to her siblings' concerns and create ridicule, especially from Neala, who had grown overprotective of her daughter.

That afternoon, as she settled Lisa down for a nap and listened to her radio programs in the kitchen, she reentered the nursery later only to find Lisa once again talking to something at the window. She ran from the room, summoning her younger brother Bobby, who took the child away from the nursery.

He brought Lisa upstairs instead, into his study – his father's former lab. There, the child played with her dolls, content to be in the company of her favorite uncle, who hovered at the drafting board. Training to become an architect, Bobby was busy drawing the elevation of a residential home for one of his architectural courses, his bed positioned where the lab jars used to be.

Bobby will never forget how his little niece mistook him for her deceased father in his funeral attire, which she had never seen. As he watched the child play, he also noted she was talking to something unseen at his window.

9. DETLIN AND DESMOND

As Neala continued to grapple with the loss of Ernest and the admonitions of her in-laws to maintain contact for the sake of Lisa, a new and dark presence made itself felt in the San Juan home. Already replete with the ghosts of the Japanese soldiers and other unblessed atrocities prior to Roberto's departure, the house became even darker, morbid, and began to meet with misfortune.

On a late afternoon in August with a monsoon rain just passed, Lisa was once again playing in her bedroom window below Roberto's former laboratory. In their haste to move back to the Lourdes Drive home, Adelaida had sought a measure of privacy for her newly widowed daughter and grandchild. She had assigned her grandchild to the small bedroom in the back of the home since it was conveniently adjacent to a bustling kitchen, where they could quickly check on her when necessary. However, the room's proximity presented a challenge in the growing twilight, for it was only a few feet from the sinister backyard.

The servant who had encountered the nameless tattered man who confronted her as she attempted to feed the cats had long abandoned her post. A new maid, Muling, young at fifteen, had now joined the family. Neala, busy now with her career and with the men who became respectable suitors, would not foresee the events to follow.

Lonely for the company of children her age, which was only available during kindergarten classes, Lisa stopped her play when the two beings once again climbed up on the windowsill. "Detlin" wore a brown outfit like a hunting vest and matching brown pants, and the other, "Desmond", was similarly garbed. They wore what appeared to be hats with a pointed top, like elves of old. Standing about four inches tall, the two beings were jolly, chuckling and busy stacking what appeared as gold plates, much larger than themselves. One appeared to be subservient to the other, as he carried the "plates" to the sill at the other's behest.

The beings chattered merrily, talking to each other as they busily stacked one "plate" after the other from an unseen source below the sill. Lisa watched, her attention held by the two happy beings, who engaged her with their busy chatter.

As the afternoon progressed, Lisa was pulled from the window by concerned aunts and uncles, who finally told Adelaida of the window "events". They were terrified that something akin to the creature that haunted Ernest had returned. They wondered if Lisa was talking to her father from beyond the grave or if something malevolent was visiting the child. However, they sensed this was very different, as Lisa did not show alarm as she had with the specter that had haunted Ernest. She was drawn to the two little beings that only she could see.

Adelaida, weary of the mysterious events, counseled her children to pray for the child. She wondered whether the creatures were somehow connected to the strange "light" that had burned her face and arms weeks before. A staunch Roman

Catholic in a country that was 99% Roman Catholic, Adelaida once again went to mass and consulted the parish priest. Still bristling from the priest's refusal to allow her son-in-law's viewing at her own parish church, she was reluctant to tell him of the encounter she'd had with the "moon" that burned her, feeling she would meet with ridicule. However, once again fearing for her granddaughter, she told him again of the sinister winged being that had led to Ernest's suicide and how she was concerned that it might have followed the child and her mother from Little Baguio.

The priest concluded there were evil spirits at the house and agreed that the evil that sent Ernest to commit suicide could easily have followed his family to Adelaida's house. She asked him to come – this time to the house on Lourdes Drive. He agreed this time with some urgency, recalling how the last event had turned to tragedy when he'd waited the weekend.

Adelaida went home, uneasy. She spent the afternoon deep in thought as she continued to dab a lotion for burns on her face. She decided to walk to the local healer, who was frequented by Aling Tale, the new laundry woman. Aware of the tragic events that permeated the household, Aling Tale had sat with Adelaida during her afternoon break weeks before, to recommend the healer should her face remain unhealed of the mysterious burns. "Shamans", or local "manghihilot", are people who are believed and trusted to provide relief when a medical or spiritual condition seems to persist. The locals, reluctant to spend so much for a medical doctor, would go first to this healer, who has shown much better results with their natural poultices and tea-leaf drinks to provide permanent healing. She felt they had nothing to lose, as she had grown to trust Aling Tale and, later, the healer, who would have been burned as a witch if they were in another country.

She appeared at the woman's shack at the edge of the neigh-

borhood, looking like a fish out of water, as she was well over-
dressed for the shanty-type dwellings on that end of the street.
The locals knew her well, however, and came to her when they
needed the intervention of a medically trained professional,
such as her husband or herself. Their reputation in the community paid off, and she was always welcomed, as she was that day.

When she offered her granddaughter's description of the
beings at the window, the manghihilot, flattered that a woman
trained in conventional medicine had come to her door, ushered
Adelaida to her simple parlor with one window overlooking the
noisy street children who played nearby. Dressed in a plain
housedress, well-worn but clean from several hand washings,
the woman believed there were "nature spirits", which existed to
watch over the trees and plants. She believed they were gnomes
or elves, part of God's creation. They were harmless unless their
dwellings were disturbed. Adelaida strained to recall any
mounds or small hills in the backyard that might have been
unwittingly dug over in her own ministrations of her plants.

Still tanned from her "event" a few weeks before, Adelaida
returned home with a poultice for her burns. That afternoon,
she walked the backyard, searching for "elfin mounds" that
might have been unintentionally disturbed. She sat and
watched Lisa at play in her nursery, waiting for her to start
talking to the invisible playmates. The aunts and uncles took
turns watching. Even Adelaida's first cousins and friends tried to
spend time with the child, observing her at play whenever they
visited. She was perfectly normal and showed a precocity for
drawing cheerful landscapes and animals, which implied a child
who was happy despite the recent tragedy.

The parish priest came after Sunday mass and walked the
entire house from top to bottom, waving a baton of holy water.
He told Neala to bring Lisa to the church every Sunday, and he
would bless her. Before he left, he made the sign of the cross on

the child's forehead and uttered a prayer. He left, not realizing that whatever was undisturbed, he had now stirred from slumber.

A few weeks passed in silence. Everyone was relieved.

Until one Friday evening.

10. THE "BEAST"

E rnest's father and mother mourned their son for the rest of their lives until they passed within months of each other. Their only grandchild was all that remained of Ernest's progeny, now a sad and shy child of five years old who had a talent for art. While still alive, the paternal grandparents attempted to include Lisa into the large family of grandchildren, inviting Neala and the child to birthday parties, fiestas and the annual Christmas party.

Lisa developed asthma shortly after her move to Adelaida's home. The illness became a standard excuse for Neala to decline any event. Overprotective of the only remaining member of her family, Neala feared the child would become ill from contact with other children. She did, however, bring her to the annual Christmas party, and the child helped Neala wrap gifts for the numerous cousins prior to the event.

Christmas was a huge and welcome event for both Ernest's and Neala's families. Festivities in the region started December 1 and ran to the feast of the Three Kings, which was January 6. In the five weeks of the season, decorations were hung from the beginning of December, and weekly parties and gatherings lasted throughout December and past New Year's.

Lisa's birthday, which was in January, was another major event, which coincided with the birthday of Adelaida's oldest, Sonya, who was Lisa's favorite aunt. The young woman, who would later move to the United States, doted on her niece and always felt she was her spiritual daughter. Lisa felt the same. The bond between the two fueled envy in Neala, who chastised the child well over what was suitable for the situation, so much so that the rest of the family came to Lisa's rescue.

Sonya baked highly creative and lavish cakes to celebrate Lisa's birthdays. So selfless was she that on a number of occasions, she decorated them without her own name on the cake, though their dates of birth were only hours apart. A highly creative chef and teacher, Sonya authored a recipe book of original and highly authentic Filipino recipes, including the famed "Sans Rival", a French-inspired cake of ten layers of meringue interspersed with almond slivers in layers of butter cream icing. It was Lisa's favorite.

By Lisa's sixth birthday, it was clear there was animosity between Sonya and Neala, with Lisa in the middle. The chaos and drama at the household became pronounced when Melissa once again returned to become Lisa's caretaker while Neala was at the newsroom. Melissa, who also grew to love her niece, became the scapegoat when Lisa caught a cold or when she started spending afternoons in front of the television after school. The youngest daughter, Sandy, now married, had moved from the increasingly turbulent household to her own apartment blocks away. Now distracted by her own infant daughter and her husband, she would only visit the turbulent home and its infestations when she was invited.

Strange smells, unexplained coldness, and darkness in areas of the house continued unabated during afternoons and evenings when there were no guests to liven up the home or when music had stopped. Muling, the young servant, remained loyal despite the conflict and sense of gloom. She remained with the family despite the sense that she was being watched whenever she entered the backyard or the more silent parts of the house. She did her best to avoid these areas and even enlisted Lisa to accompany her on chores. Once done, the two would madly dash out of the area with nervous laughter as soon as a chore was done. It almost became a game.

Into the conflicted San Juan home came a new haunting whose origins can only be traced back to the blessing done a few years ago when Lisa had been visited by Detlin and Desmond. One late afternoon as twilight grew in the house, Lisa was alone by the window overlooking the side yard. The two beings had now for several months not made an appearance at the other window, to the family's relief. The window facing the side yard had an adjacent laundry area where the gaunt man had been seen by the previous maid.

Muling felt "watched" once the sun had set and finally after Adelaida confronted her as to why Lisa always came along with her to the upstairs rooms, Muling refused to go altogether. However, Adelaida gave in to the maid's proposed cleaning schedule, as the family was having difficulty keeping servants in the home. Muling reported seeing "things" standing at the periphery of her vision as she would walk past a room or as she turned; she felt something shift to get away from her line of sight. So it came to pass that she would only clean and dust the rooms during the morning when the sun graced the rooms of their gloom. At night, she left the lights on in her alcove by the stairs, afraid something or someone would walk up the steps and "greet" her as she tried to sleep.

One afternoon, Roberto Sr. was visiting the house and was invited to stay for dinner by his sons. Though Adelaida did not approve of his stay, she kept quiet about it, as Roberto would give his sons an allowance and even spend time with them, which they needed. As was his custom when he lived there, the aging doctor sat in the drawing room to watch one of his favorite programs, which happened to be a horror series, coming on at 7 p.m. before the dinner hour. This was before the time of "prime time" when shows that were objectionable for viewing by children still came on earlier in the evening.

As Lisa emerged from her bedroom, she entered the drawing room as the opening credits started to roll on the television. She stopped, appalled to see the image of a silhouette on the TV screen, and ran in terror from the room. The opening credits showed a man walking precariously through a dark forest, the backdrop eerie, the theme music haunting. Roberto turned to find a concerned Muling asking him to turn it down.

Adelaida came out of the kitchen with Melissa to follow Lisa into the dining room, where she crawled right next to her aunt Sonya, trembling. She told them it was a "moo moo", a ghost on the TV screen. Roberto joined them and told them of the program. He consoled the child and told them he had changed the channel. Later, Roberto told the family that Lisa must have been either traumatized by her father's death or have an overactive imagination.

Sonya sat the child by her elbow at the table to keep her company. Dinner went uneventfully, as Roberto's sons were told to keep quiet about the incident, afraid it would scare the child even more. Roberto departed right after dinner when Neala came home. Melissa escorted Lisa to her room, as it was getting late, and prepared her for bed. As she exited the room, the child climbed up on the windowsill, playing with her toy kitchen.

As Lisa arranged the small cups and plates on the cupboard and sink, mimicking her grandmother and Muling, she detected someone standing just outside of view outside the window to her right. Curious, she observed the darkness through the mesh screen. Suddenly, she saw a silhouette of a man in profile. She smelled cigarette smoke, the scent familiar to her. It dawned on her it was her father's scent of tobacco when he smoked. Knowing by that age that he had passed, she started to move away when the smoke started wafting through the window screen.

A feeling of sadness and menace was palpable in the room.

Suddenly, the shadow disappeared.

Lisa screamed and fell back onto the bed.

Melissa ran into the room, followed by Sonya and Bobby.

The next day, the parish priest walked through the house, blessing every corner of every room. He asked Neala to bring the child to him at the church again.

On a warm Sunday morning before mass, Neala brought Lisa to the rectory, where a priest blessed the child and gave her a certificate that made her, in the church's eyes, baptized again.

It would be the final time she would see a church until she took an overseas voyage to permanently leave the haunted home.

11. FLIGHT

I n 1972 martial law took its oppressive grip on Manila and the Philippines at large. Neala, who still remained within the society of fellow journalists, became concerned about her position as a prominent copyrighter. She openly rebelled against the existing regime, which was now on the hunt for people who did not support Marcos. Individuals in media started to "disappear" and sometimes were found shot or meeting an accident.

Guerrilla forces descended into the jungles, hiding and re-arming themselves in a plan to overthrow the increasingly powerful despot at Malacanang Palace. As the number of rebel forces increased from all walks of life, their families fled, fearful of reprisal. Neala, idealistic and outspoken, attempted to assist the underground groups. She had left journalism for an advertising career, but despite the change, she kept in touch with her colleagues from the paper, so she was privy to more and more news of government corruption, which came from her sources.

Since the increase of strange and terrifying events in her daughter's bedroom, Neala had moved the child to the upstairs room near her aunt Sonya, leaving the nursery as a storage area.

It was in the new bedroom where Neala would allow her fellow journalists who went into hiding a night or two of shelter after Sonya departed for a position in the US. Rifles, ammunition and other related paraphernalia would be stashed under the child's bed where no one would suspect a young girl's room to hold an arsenal.

Adelaida's growing fear of being discovered that they were aiding the rebels made for even more conflict in the turbulent home. Curtains drawn and conversations hushed to low tones made for tense evenings with the comings and goings of strangers with weapons. Neala's siblings avoided the house, but felt trapped at nightfall with the strict curfew imposed by the regime. When they returned, they would find strange men sharing the dinner table with a tense Muling standing by. It was during this time that Lisa would find herself almost losing her mother, when Neala went into hiding with the guerrillas for three weeks.

As the government attempted to rout out the journalists and professors who fought against them, soldiers went after family members to make individuals surrender. At Saint Paul's, the private school where Lisa was a student, soldiers marched in through the school's gates by order of their superior. The nuns, terrified, took every child who had a parent suspect and hid them.

One late morning, as recess drew to a close, Lisa sat in the classroom near one of the open arches, which gave her a view of the vast corridor of the large school. She loved her classroom seat, as it afforded her a cool breeze from the corridors, which had windows open to the shady trees. Suddenly, she heard the gates in the distance all open and a shout yelled out from a man of authority. The marching of boots in the distance volleyed down the school's driveways. A sense of apprehension and expectation invaded the classroom of fifty students. The teacher, a laywoman in her forties, paused and asked the students to hush as a nun in a habit dashed into the room. Several nuns trotted with urgency down the vast hallway.

Saint Paul's, a Roman Catholic school, which had primary to secondary grades housed in Spanish-style buildings with red tile roofs, also had a large college in the rear of the compound adjacent to the cloister and cemetery. The school had been founded by French nuns from the order of Saint Paul of Chartres. It was in this school where nuns, still in traditional garb, would time and again rush to their students' side in an effort to shield them from the outside world, which was in the midst of political upheaval.

Sister Gemma dashed to Lisa's side, entering one of the side archways as the nun in front addressed the class. She asked Lisa to quickly come with her. As they exited the room, they were met by the Mother Superior, who ushered Lisa down the hall and into a communicating corridor. At one of the lockers, she paused and leaned down to the child of eleven.

"I am going to ask you to go in there." She pointed to the open locker. "I need you to be very quiet and not come out until someone like me opens the locker."

Lisa nodded anxiously.

"Do not move or make a sound. Do you have a cough or cold?"

"No."

"Are you sure?"

"Yes."

Quickly, another nun appeared, and they pushed Lisa into the small beige locker, where she sat with her arms and legs folded.

"Remember, whatever you hear, do not make a sound."

Lisa nodded.

The locker clicked shut.

Boots marched, a scattering of booted feet, then men shouting orders.

Voices approached as boots came closer.

Booted feet walked by.

One stopped.

An intake of breath.

Lisa held her own breath, now sweating profusely with fear.

The feet moved on.

The afternoon grew dark. Then, finally, a nun unlatched the lock and knocked.

Lisa emerged, unfolding her cramped legs. She was handed a glass of water.

As the private bus dropped Lisa off at the corner of Lourdes Drive, she exited and ran quickly down the street, wondering why the small bus didn't stop at her grandmother's gate.

As she neared the residence, she watched a large jeep pass near her. Submachine guns crowned the top of the jeep, with two men in army garb standing behind them.

She noted men standing lined up against the wall of the Mastrile compound, adjacent to the neighbors' across the street.

Suddenly, the jeep paused midway to idle right where the line of men stood in wait. The two men opened fire.

Rat-tat-tat-tat-tat –

Blood jetted out of each man, who all dropped one by one in front of the canal. The wall turned red, and the smell of ripe grapes assailed Lisa's nose. She ran for her grandmother's house, just yards from the dying men.

Three more steps and she reached the gate. The iron gate's door had a hole larger than a quarter.

It was obvious something had occurred right outside her grandmother's house. Lisa pushed, to find the iron gate ajar, giving way with a shriek. She entered the driveway, the silence jolting her heart.

In terror, she entered the house, searching for what she thought might be bodies of her family. She heard her dog, a Valentine's gift when she was nine, whimper from the kitchen.

"Scamp?"

The small dog exited from the back of the refrigerator.

She leaned down to reach for the dog and saw her grandmother folded under the dining table.

"Oh, thank God you're here!" Adelaida leaped out and ran to Lisa's side, protectively enfolding her.

"Where's Tita?" (Melissa).

They ran upstairs to find Melissa hidden behind the army trunk of solid wood. The window seat's edge where she had been just moments ago had the mark of a bullet.

In the back of the house, they discovered Roberto Senior lying flat on the floor, waiting.

"Roberto, they're gone."

He rose and joined them.

Two weeks later, Neala reappeared at the house and packed their bags.

They flew to Hawaii, then LA. Lisa toured Disneyland, her memories still filled with the scent of ripe grapes. In her new jacket pocket, a photo of Scamp, the pet dog she'd left behind.

12. CONNECTICUT

Neala left Lisa in the New England town of New Haven, famous for the campus of Yale University, as it is today. Lisa ended at her aunt Sonya's doorstep upon arrival that spring evening. Sonya had left the haunted family home, getting away from family and friends of her youth a few years before Marcos had declared martial law in the once prosperous country. Leaving in the wake of economic decline and political freedom, Neala proceeded to New York City with hopes of starting a new career at a new advertising agency. Armed with her high recommendations and the blessing of a friend who was local in one of New York's ad agencies, she hoped to reestablish the flourishing career she'd had while in Manila.

Sonya had awaited Lisa with great anticipation in New Haven. Neala's older sister had moved to accept a job at Yale and lived minutes within the center of campus. In the '70s, Yale was ensconced within a charming and quaint small town with thriving businesses. A typical New England town, New Haven had a town center with a "town green", or park, where three churches stood grand within yards of each other. Surrounding the green, businesses such as the local post office, the leading bank, doctors, attorneys and shops faced the charming and quiet central square, where people converged and strolled. Women walked dogs and pushed strollers while elderly couples ate confections and pensioners played chess.

Indeed, as the name suggests, it was a "haven" for professors, artists and writers, who frequented Yale not only for employment but also for its enriched atmosphere that only a college town can bring. Yale welcomed foreign visitors, students with visas, anyone who sought education and culture. Close by, Italian, Polish and Irish immigrants from post-war Europe converged and plied their artisan shops, recreating the culture of their birth. It was a new beginning in a thriving college town just minutes from the Atlantic coast.

At the nearby mall, department stores opened early and closed late, providing an air-conditioned haven in the hot summers and a respite from the frost in winters. Within the department stores such as Edward Malley, Macy's and the local Kresge's, restaurants and pharmacies served lunch for two dollars, egg creams for ten cents, and sundaes for thirty-five cents. Women sewed. The local Woolworth's down the street held fabrics for dresses, gowns and curtains. Patterns for the latest fashion were on sale such as Butterick's.

Inside the eighth floor of a high-rise apartment building where Sonya shared a large flat with two other single women from her native country, the reunion with Sonya was a joyous occasion. Missing friends and other family members, Lisa shed her shyness and, despite the age difference, charmed and befriended Sonya's two roommates, who were immigrants themselves. They all worked for Yale University as professionals in different departments – and were eager to introduce Lisa to the educationally and culturally rich environment that a university town had to offer.

Lisa enrolled in a private school for girls and for several

months missed her friends at Saint Paul's. Saint Mary's, a small Dominican school with very conservative nuns, embraced her as the first Asian child to enroll there. Eventually, she garnered friends from the town but found their ideas way too conformist, and she sought outlets against the puritanical environment of the small high school. Not unlike her father, she started writing poetry and, like Sonya, started reading books. Among the classics, Sonya was drawn to the paranormal after being raised in a haunted home. Lisa followed suit, choosing books from shelves that were not normal fare for a teenage child. Books such as *Seth Speaks*, Edgar Cayce's works, Ruth Montgomery and any book she could find on the afterlife, as well as ESP, came to her awareness. Sonya – always a believer in reincarnation, the transmigration of souls, psychic power and multidimensionality – shared with Lisa her treasured collection in her living room's small library. Eventually, Lisa extended her search to the university stacks and the bookstores within the community and, eventually, New York City.

As her first year in Connecticut drew to a close with the end of winter, Lisa excelled in high school, finding the curriculum easy despite the conservative atmosphere lent by the presence of the nuns. However, every moment she had free, she trolled the school library's stacks for those books that opened for her a new set of eyes. When she found little, she went to the public library and exhausted their outdated collection. Finally, she approached her aunt and her friends, who gave her access to Sterling Library at Yale. There, a panoply of books on Buddhism, Taoism, Transcendental Meditation and all things related to support her growing desire to look deeper into the nature of the spirit became available.

It was in this atmosphere as a novice in meditation where Lisa started practicing creative visualization. She discovered astral projection, the precursor to remote viewing, which was still in its infancy in the early '70s. As her meditative practices became routine, she decided to consciously focus on transporting herself psychically into different corners of the streets below, standing on the balcony of the eighth-floor apartment. She attempted to visualize what the features of a particular street corner looked like as if she were there, turning 360 degrees. She familiarized herself with the landmarks in "real" time, then would mentally "walk" down a street, concentrating on the feel of the pavement, the buildings and the details of shop storefronts. It was as if she had the precursor to the app Google Street View, which materialized several decades later.

Eventually, Lisa shared this practice with one or two close friends whom she thought she could trust. To her chagrin, the two girls thought it was "odd" and started distancing themselves. She hoped that one day, she could mentally teleport herself to a location and witness events from afar while her body comfortably rested at home. Lisa had the beginnings of wanderlust.

One evening, while asleep in the bedroom, which she shared with Sonya, she felt her body begin to rise. Lisa awakened to find herself with her nose an inch from the ceiling. The sensation, so sudden, terrified her. Immediately, she found herself back on the bed. Thinking she was perhaps dreaming, she threw it up to wishful thinking. Until the following week.

One afternoon, just home from school, Lisa wandered off to the public library. There, she found a book and borrowed it. Upon her return home, she sat on the living room carpet, opened the book, and read the directions. Sitting in a lotus position, she closed her eyes and concentrated on floating up to the ceiling. In a few minutes, in a meditative state, she heard something "click" within her and felt a distinct sensation of moving up. She felt her body stay seated on the carpet, but she felt her consciousness begin to elevate above her body. She looked up as the ceiling started to come closer, the light fixture becoming larger.

Willing herself not to be afraid, as she knew she had a "silver cord" and was in good health at age fourteen, she allowed her internal being to rise. She rose a few inches, feeling a very light, fluid sensation akin to an inflated balloon. Then Molly, her aunt's roommate, came home.

She psychically felt her own presence slide back into her body, as if she had slipped on ice. Molly smiled at her as she sat cross-legged on the carpet. A staid Catholic, the older woman thought Lisa was praying as she sat across from a small bookcase, which held an altar.

The next night, as her aunt fell asleep, Lisa tried again. This time, as she rose toward the ceiling, she mentally willed herself to look back at the bed. There, in her frilled flannel nightgown, lay her body on the bed, asleep, eyelids shut in rapid movement. She turned back to look up as her face entered the ceiling and her being rose faster and higher until she found herself staring at the open sky of night. Afraid of getting lost, she willed herself to return to the apartment, where she ended up in the dining room opposite the kitchen.

By the window, she noted a copper bowl with ornate filigree, new to her. She attempted to reach for it with curiosity, but she noted she could not. The scent of jasmine came from the bowl, which calmed her. She willed herself to go back to the room.

She awakened the next day, a Saturday. As she approached the breakfast table, she saw the copper bowl with the filigree design. Approaching it while Molly chatted with Sonya, she smelled the distinct scent of jasmine. The hairs on her arms stood up as she realized the previous night's journey had not been a dream.

13. THE HAUNTINGS AT SAINT PAUL'S

F ive years later, now a US citizen and martial law finally lifted, Neala ventured to visit. Flying back with Lisa in tow, who was now entering university, Neala reunited with friends from the ad agency, now realizing the flight to the United States was a major career nosedive. In the early '70s, as it still is in some areas of the US, the discrimination and marginalization of immigrants from Asian and South American countries was palpable, if not downright hostile.

All previous training and experience was usually discounted from the émigré's country of origin. To her chagrin, Neala felt pigeonholed as an Asian woman from a third world country. Indeed, even the following era still remained for her an experience punctuated by prejudice, as she was to discover by remaining in the east coast.

Disillusioned by her flight but still hopeful to regain her former status in the circles of Manila, Neala visited and reunited with her mother and siblings. Nieces and nephews had been born in her and Lisa's absence, though a few were already young children when she and Lisa left in 1973.

The self-imposed exile to a foreign country did nothing to

increase Neala's sense of safety. Lisa, now completing high school and accepted as a freshman at a Jesuit university in Connecticut, was reluctant to return to her country of origin, unsure of what another major change would bring. Too young to foresee the ramifications of living in a foreign country, she would later encounter, in middle age, locals who coveted her position and envied her lifestyle, which she'd won from decades of hard work and self-sacrifice.

Despite Neala's difficulties grappling with the reality of a career now lost to others, and the journalists gone who had helped her reach the pinnacle of her career, it was not for naught. It was during this two-month visit back to San Juan that Lisa would discover the culture she had not forgotten, but actually pined for in her early years at Saint Mary's. It was also an epiphany to her in more ways than she could imagine when she visited the sites of her childhood with new eyes.

Meeting up with elementary friends, Lisa visited her alma mater, which had grown in size since her absence. Most of her friends had stayed to attend the high school in the same complex but dispersed to other friendships as their interests changed. Even her best friend had changed much in the interim. Touring the school with the eyes of a seventeen-year-old, she heard stories from her former teachers, including the groundskeeper, who told her of the school's haunted halls. Now well-read on the topic of ghosts, the afterlife, ESP, telepathy, karma and the tenets of reincarnation, Lisa was not intimidated by the topic nor was she fearful of ghosts and the like. They were not as "unknown" to her as when she was a child. Thus, she was eager to hear details of stories that she'd avoided or unwittingly missed while she had been a student there.

The school's chapel, built of cement and stone in Spanish colonial style, was a two-floor affair with stained-glass windows bracketing the entire second floor. The two balconies on either side of the chapel opened to the main altar below and the congregation seating. It was in this chapel that several students and a number of teachers would recount the specter that they avoided as the day wore on to evening.

The school, known for its patronage of orphans, took a few in who were indigent and raised them to become educated. Some orphans chose to stay and become novice sisters of Saint Paul, some went into teaching, and some departed for other careers outside the cloister.

One orphan child in particular, whom I will name "Gwen", assisted elderly nuns while she attended school. Living in a dormitory near the infirm nuns of the order, she did chores and assisted the sisters when everyone else left for the day to go home to their families. She was close to the teachers, as she, unlike the other students, only had the clothes on her back and whatever the sisters of the order gave her for food, shelter and an allowance. It was during these times when she visited with teachers and fellow students that she told us her stories as a "living tenant" of the school.

One of the chores Gwen had was to carry trays of food back and forth from the elementary school's large canteen, which had one department devoted to preparing meals for the teaching staff as well as the nuns in residence. Mealtimes were straddled between the elementary recess and lunch and the schedule for the secondary grades. The girl was assigned to the canteen to pick up breakfast for the bed-ridden nuns before school's opening when teachers came for breakfast and dinner after all the students and lay teachers were dismissed. At the end of the day, Gwen had the privilege of partaking of any cakes and snacks left from the college in the rear of the school, which had the best canteen.

Schools in the Philippines had long days. Elementary and secondary students began at 6:45 a.m. promptly so that the parents could drop them off prior to going to work. They could opt to go home for lunch, which was an hour and a half long, attended by their grandparents and servants. School continued again at one and ended at 4:15 for the first to seventh grades. The high school students started and ended later. Gwen's shift thus began early before sunrise with the cleaning of the canteen, feeding of the chickens, and tending the farm garden behind the college buildings. She stopped work to attend school and began again at six after all the students departed.

One early morning around 4 a.m., Gwen awakened in the dark dormitory and began her day. She watered the vegetable garden outside the dorm, fed the chickens, and washed herself before reporting to the Mother Superior. Armed with a tray, she proceeded down the dark hallway and climbed the stairs, taking a short cut through the chapel where the Mother Superior usually prayed before she began her day. Gwen needed to take the woman's breakfast request before all the others.

Dressed in the school's uniform, she entered the chapel and peered down from the second floor, with the stained-glass windows behind her. She noted the altar lights were off, which meant the nuns had not prepared it for the matins. She wondered if the Mother Superior had left for a meeting. Quickly, she walked down the dark hall, in search of the Mother Superior on her way to the canteen. The only light she had was from whatever light came through the stained-glass windows to her right, which wasn't much at that early morning hour.

Ahead of her, she noticed a nun in a black habit walking ahead. She thought it was funny she had not seen her before and now hastened her steps to catch up and inquire.

"Hello, *po. Magandang umaga, po.*" (Hello and good morning, ma'am.)

Gwen was met with silence as the nun ahead continued walking.

"Do you know if Sister Gemma is away today?"

Gwen paused for a reply, but the nun kept walking.

Gwen followed, miffed as she tried to identify the rude nun who ignored her.

As she moved to catch up, the nun turned as the hall ended, toward the organ.

Gwen stopped, now noticing the nun had NO feet, but was floating as she turned.

Ahead of Gwen, the nun floated, then turned toward her. She had no face inside the habit.

Gwen dropped the tray and ran headlong for the exit door.

News of this specter spread as more nuns encountered the "silent nun", who floated on the upper floor of the chapel. It was speculated by teachers who talked of the sighting in the faculty dining room that a young nun had jumped to her death onto the lower chapel from that balcony after hearing she was pregnant.

Another event happened when the students in seventh grade happened upon the school's cemetery, where the elderly nuns were buried. As a student there, Lisa had a large group of friends who made it a regular outing to explore the school's campus.

It was in seventh grade that Lisa's group of friends, now more than a dozen, decided to go on an "expedition" after school to verify the groundskeeper's gossip about a recently interred priest whose body disappeared after burial. The story went that the family was very distraught to find that their brother and son had somehow been stolen from the ground after burial. But why?

Behind the secondary school grounds where the high school students attended classes, the college's manicured lawns began. Separated by a garden, the college had an arts building and a sciences building. If you walked past the garden, a small open area began where the rectory was located and a shop and dormitory for the gardening and maintenance staff. Behind these buildings, a path began that led to the most remote and least developed area of the complex: the cemetery for departed clergy.

A sense of loneliness and abandonment lent an aura of isolation to the tended, but modest headstones, some as old as pre-war Manila. The nuns who lived out their lives at the cloister in various jobs remained until their death. In these few acres of ground, their headstones lay flat on the ground, lined modestly without fancy carvings or lettering. Lisa gingerly followed her friends at the time, reluctant to see the empty grave, which had become the topic of the month. Why the curiosity? There were more ghosts at home, she declared.

As students in groups dared each other to visit the cemetery, whose location was unknown to them prior to the teachers' gossip, Rita, the oldest of Lisa's friends, ventured the idea. By day's end, a plan had been hatched and the location of the cemetery identified. Eight of the twelve friends elected to stay after school and miss the private bus home.

Rita led the curious gaggle of seventh graders, the most courageous of the friends, to the path leading to the cemetery. The open grave was situated closer to the school's high twelve-foot cement wall, which was the campus' west end. Thus, the open grave was in darkness, the wall lending a shadow to the remote spot.

As the students gingerly watched right and left for the staff, who would surely shoo them away, they passed the maintenance shed and finally reached the short fence that marked the cemetery. They entered in single file, Rita in front, the pack leader, and Victoria, the most reluctant, in the rear. Lisa was behind Rita, anxious to run if anyone stirred from the graves. She hoped that her grandmother Adelaida, who waited anxiously at home, did not hear of this adventure. She was supposedly tutoring the younger students in reading music.

Ahead, blue tarp marked the fringes of the open grave, and a large mound of dirt was packed next to the pit like a hill. They stepped forward, peering at the bottom, hoping to spot some sign of the casket. The grave was empty.

"Ha ha. Did you think you'd find anything there?!"

Stunned by the unexpected voice, the girls turned.

An old man with a worn pair of khaki pants and a shirt stained with dirt and paint, obviously part of the maintenance crew, smiled with stained teeth. His hair was plastered with sweat, his face suntanned and lined with age.

Rita stammered, "We-we were just trying to verify what the teachers told us... for an English paper!"

The man chuckled, relaxed. "It's okay. I'm Mang Tino."

The girls sheepishly smiled in their uniforms, glancing at each other for cues.

Mang Tino (Mr. Tino) proceeded to inform them: "I've tried to bury the coffin about four times now... in two weeks."

Victoria spoke up, unable to resist. "Where IS the coffin?"

The old man laughed. "Gone. No one knows where. But I tried to close that grave... but it keeps getting dug up!"

The girls collectively looked back at the open grave, some peering in.

"You see that mound of dirt there?"

They nodded.

"It wasn't there yesterday! I had covered up the pit!

"Or the day before!" he added with a look of mischief.

Rita queried, trying to verify: "So you can't find the body, and you can't cover the pit?!"

Mang Tino nodded, winking. "Strange, huh? It keeps opening up."

An eerie wind blew as the sun began to set. The area was

now in twilight. The girls stood in a circle with growing unease, deciding what to do.

Rita ventured: "Let's go."

She turned to thank Mang Tino, but he was gone. Had he walked away? Terror gripped them. The girls ran all the way back to the college garden, sitting on a bench to compose themselves. It was time to go home. When Lisa visited Saint Paul's as a college freshman, the entire school had expanded. New buildings had been built where the gardens had been. She dared not venture back to the cemetery where the open grave might be. But curious, she did.

Nothing was quite the same. The aura of isolation in the rear of the campus was gone, replaced by a parking lot for faculty. She could not locate the cemetery or the lonely path that led to the open grave.

14. DINNER AT THE SAMPALOC HOUSE

An hour outside Manila was a bustling neighborhood of old homes. Ernest's parents had raised all eleven children in this neighborhood, all highly educated, cosmopolitan and successful in their adult years. As the aging parents enjoyed their years with their married children and grandchildren, one among them was missing and so was his only child.

When Neala visited with Lisa, it was with great anticipation of a reunion with Lisa's paternal grandparents. Most of Ernest's siblings had relocated to Europe and the US. A few held positions in diplomacy, some as ambassadors to foreign countries. However, Ernest's older brother chose to bring his new wife to live with his parents as a way of watching over them in their elder years. By the time Neala and daughter arrived, it was only that couple who resided in the house with their father. At this point, his young wife, Mina, was with child, and Lisa's paternal grandmother had passed away.

Despite the bustling street outside the grandparents' home, it was relatively quiet inside. A large living room commanded the front of the house, and then a double door connected it to the large dining room, where the entire family could all dine around a large antique table made of "nara", a heavy tropical wood of high quality. In the time of the family's youth, all the children gathered around their parents to dine at this table every evening. The large kitchen in back opened to an outdoor pantry where the servants slaughtered fresh chickens newly bought from the open market with fresh vegetables and the day's fish.

Lisa was warmly welcomed by an uncle she hardly knew and an aunt she recalled meeting a few times before their exodus. The grandfather, Padring, was now in his eighties and walked with a cane. As the visit wore on, the family decided to share dinner together at the house. As the meal was being prepared, Mina, still making acquaintances with Lisa, brought out some old photos of the family. Among them was Ernest's old photos when he was a child and then as a teen.

As the group waited for dinner, they all moved to the large dining room, where Mina continued to show the family's old albums and photos on the large table. Along one wall of the dining room was a series of windows, all shut to prevent the harsh sunlight from shining in, which made the room extremely hot. As the conversation became livelier, Mina brought out a piece of paper that she showed to Lisa. It was her father's death certificate, which Lisa had never seen.

As a small child and later as an adolescent, no one had revealed to Lisa how Ernest had died. She was told Ernest smoked a lot and died of emphysema. Along with the bizarre looks and side glances she received when he was discussed, Lisa knew it was a cover-up. Neala, who had attempted to shield her from the dark and sinister past they'd shared together the first few years in Little Baguio, was content to leave the subject alone.

Now, sitting at her grandparents' dining table, her deceased father's sister-in-law, unaware of Lisa's lack of knowledge, placed the certificate in Lisa's hands. Lisa looked down, and a chill ran over her. There, in print, was the method of death by exsanguination. He had bled out by cutting his own wrists.

Suddenly, Lisa looked up at Mina, the hairs on her arms rising, a humming in her ears. The room grew mysteriously cold and silent. All these years when queried by classmates and nosy teachers why her father was absent, she offered that he had committed suicide by cutting his wrists. Now, in black and white on the table the paper before her showed her explanation was true. How did she come to know, as no one was courageous enough to tell her the truth about him on either side of the family?

Neala inched over as she saw Lisa's face, the conversation coming to a halt between her in-laws and her. She looked down at the paper and took it away from Lisa. Mina, stunned at the implication, exclaimed guiltily that she didn't know.

Neala looked at her daughter, turning pale, dreading her reaction. To her surprise, Lisa indicated she had always known the stories were lies, and she was shocked that what she thought was true. The in-laws all looked at each other in silence. Suddenly, as if on cue, all the shutters opened in unison to the twilight. A huge swarm of cockroaches assailed the family as they sat at the table. A maid, who'd just entered with a pot of stew, ran back to the kitchen as the cockroaches attacked the dining table, darkening the entire room. Padring yelled for a broom, and an elderly maid entered, swatting right and left at the cockroaches, who were now swarming all over the dining table and covering the photographs. Lisa ran from the room to the safety of the second-floor bedrooms. Mina followed, swatting the cockroaches as she went. Neala bolted with her elderly father-in-law for the safety of the kitchen, where they waited, appalled. Then, as suddenly as the swarm appeared, the cockroaches fled from the room, only a few dead from the servants' efforts to subdue them. The brother-in-law swatted away what remained of the large insects, stunned.

As Lisa went down the steps with Mina, who looked as pale as a ghost, she asked Lisa, "How did you know?" Later, Lisa would discuss this with a seer, who told her that the swarm was a sign of the evil that triumphed when Ernest killed himself.

15. NEW YORK

Lisa returned to the US and spent her final few weeks of summer before moving to the dorm by visiting with her mother, who lived in Queens. The previous summers, Neala had introduced her to a self-proclaimed seer, "Beth" – a woman in her thirties who read palms and auras in the privacy of her home. In her cozy and comfortable apartment house in the hamlet of Elmhurst, decorated with icons of saints, the Buddha and other sacred masters still unknown to Lisa, the woman did a reading. Beth told Lisa that she saw her as an "old soul" who had been through several lives as far back as 1066 in several countries, even as a male American Indian in the southwest.

Fueled by recurring dreams of lives populated by current relatives and "people" she did not know but knew well in the dreams, Lisa was determined to find an explanation for why her father had exited the current life at such a young age, albeit due to the specter that had infested the home in Little Baguio. Among the relatives she had recurring dreams about, continuous and vivid full-color dreams, he was mysteriously absent. She wondered if Beth could shed light on her father, who'd become the topic at the Sampaloc house after the infestation of cockroaches.

Intrigued by the purpose of her recurring dreams, which showed events as if from a movie, Lisa was driven to piece together what brought her to the current lifetime. Did her efforts to have an out-of-body experience have some connection, or did her outright curiosity about the afterlife bring on dream after dream? Lisa kept having dreams of a life in parts of Europe. Particular houses and people she knew in waking life looked very different in the lifetimes shown to her in full color. They were so vivid she could smell the field of flowers during a dream in Spain, touch the water in the reflecting pool in southern France bordered by cypresses, and watch the tents ripple in the sandy wind during a life in the Middle East.

In several successive dreams, she dreamed all the family members in different roles than they were in the current lifetime. Her aunt Sonya had always told her that they shared lives as mother and daughter in previous lifetimes. Neala was Lisa's older sister in a lifetime in Spain, her uncle Bobby was a father in three lifetimes in England, and she herself drowned several times in different lifetimes. Now she knew why she was afraid of water, and the terror prevented her, even now, from learning to swim.

One late afternoon, Lisa visited with Beth, who eagerly offered her some Greek coffee – a gift from a boyfriend who'd just returned from overseas. As they settled down to catch up, Beth asked Lisa to turn her coffee cup over so that the lip touched the saucer. Lisa did so as Beth explained that the finely ground coffee beans could read the future and past of the person who drank from it. Beth reached over, took the cup, and proceeded to read it. Lisa took the little visit as a free fortune-telling "game", as Beth did not fit the role, minus the crystal ball, the bangles absent on her wrists, and the lack of incense.

The young woman Beth told her that she was being "watched" and "monitored" by "good beings" who knew about the evil that had tried to infest their home early in Lisa's lifetime. She went on to tell her that they were protecting her from the evil presence, who was intrigued by her. The unexpected revelation made Lisa uncomfortable, if not understandably alarmed.

Lisa then confessed that she had been meditating and attempting astral projection (out-of-body experiences) since she was a young teen and had almost "projected" on a few occasions, but drew back and bounced back to her body. Beth cautioned her not to try without praying first, as she was afraid "something" was close by, always watching when Lisa was unprotected. Like her father, who was kind, compassionate and pure at heart, the "evil" Beth alluded to found Lisa a challenge.

Lisa went back to her mother's apartment house, which she shared with two other roommates. That night, she prayed and did not try to project herself. However, a new type of dream assailed her. A man with flowing white robes, bearded and with piercing blue eyes, exuded benevolence in her dream. He extended his arm, fingers in benediction, towards her. Lisa felt unafraid, and a thought came to her that it was a positive spirit, even one of holiness. As the figure walked away, Lisa was overtaken by sadness; then, suddenly, she found herself in the dream on a street at night.

Lisa was fully aware she was not in her body, but that she had some type of mission. As she examined the street to determine its location, she realized she was in a street of a large city, perhaps even across the river in Manhattan itself. Garbage was piled in dumpsters and strewn in the alleys, the darkness foreboding and intimidating. The sound of traffic passing by, cars screeching, and the detritus of the day told her it was not a good area. She sensed a presence near her and found another being, much like herself in vibration, accompanying her as she "wandered" the streets. A second being nearby, she sensed, was male. Through telepathy, she got the message they were patrolling the streets and were being "mentored" by the male being.

Around the corner, by a fire escape, a fight had occurred. One man, who appeared Hispanic, fell, bleeding. Lisa darted forward to aid him and was "told" he was about to pass, as the injury was a fatal wound. As the man lay on the pavement, wet with water, his blood poured forth and mixed with the water. Lisa saw that the person became still. A dark creature, like a thick shadow, materialized from the ground nearby.

From the dead man came a white smoke wafting out of his body. The smoke, Lisa sensed, was intelligent. The dark shadow came near it. Lisa was told the smoke was the dead man's spirit, now accosted by the dark shadow. Another dark shadow appeared, hovering and cornering the spirit of the terrified man. On cue, Lisa approached with the other being next to her. She raised her "astral" hand to reach for the man's spirit, who "saw" her, and she sensed confusion. A light came from above them, the mentor. Then Lisa saw a brightness come from behind her and from the being next to her. Their collective brightness penetrated the two dark shadows, and the shadows fled in terror.

With both "arms" extended, Lisa reached for the man's spirit in an effort to embrace it. The white smoke sensed their assistance, and Lisa raised her arm, pointing upwards. The smoke, relieved, flew up and up until it was gone. The spirit companions around Lisa gave her a telepathic "smile" of triumph. They continued on to the next confrontation, entering buildings, sending spirits to the Light.

Lisa awakened to morning and joined her mother and friends for breakfast in the kitchen. As she looked out the window while her mother chatted with her roommates, she remembered the dream in vivid detail. She wondered where she had been in New York that previous night.

As summer turned to fall and Lisa moved into a dorm, the dreams started to become prolonged and complicated. She found herself in various locales where she was taken and witnessed the aftermath of conflict and crimes. Several souls, she felt, they had saved from being taken by "silhouette beings", who seemed to come up through the pavement. Her interpretation of them was religious, and she became eager to please the elderly man in the white robe, whose benevolence she craved. She surmised he was a "master" or a high being of light, close to God. Therefore, she eagerly looked forward to the dreams so that she could travel and be part of their compassionate mission, although the beings who fled were frightening.

One night, sleeping in her dorm, Lisa had a different type of "voyage". Now disinterested in astral projection by will, as it seemed to come her way via "dreams", Lisa wasn't prepared for what came next. Now away from New York in a suburb of the bedroom community of Connecticut, she couldn't easily visit with Beth, whose company she sought. She had not been able to update her on the progress of her dreams, the books she came upon, and the revelations she encountered in her night forays into a different dimension.

Few would understand her and what she had experienced. She would keep it close to her heart, knowing the college she was in was very conservative. She felt marginalized and snubbed by the students who came from certain types of families. A feeling of alienation overcame her, with only a few of her dorm mates she would be interested in calling a friend.

Sonya remained in New Haven and continued to visit her. Their relationship remained as close as ever, but Lisa did not want to trouble her aunt with details of her dreams, as she sensed conflict between her mother and the gracious aunt. With Neala now moved into a house with her older sister, the strife became a daily grind, which Lisa only heard on weekends when she returned to visit. This grind would materialize into a hateful relationship and eventually end with the death of her aunt from cancer, two weeks before her college graduation.

On a spring night, Lisa had just retired to bed and left her dorm window open to the unseasonably warm breeze. She looked forward to coming home for the summer and hoped that she could schedule a visit to Queens to catch up with Beth. Though the university was close to New York, Lisa was reluctant to take the subway alone to Queens, as crime had escalated in the city in the late '70s. She couldn't think of anyone to accompany her to see the young woman and not be ridiculed. Though she felt safe in her astral body to travel the streets at night, searching for lost souls, by day, her mortal body presented a hazard, as she was a vulnerable young woman in a large metropolitan city.

Lisa drifted off and immediately felt herself flowing out the open window. Immediately, she was seized by some force against her will and felt herself go past clouds and higher than she had been before. The stars appeared much brighter than before. Ahead of her, she saw her aunt Sonya beckoning. She too appeared in a nightgown, such as she would have worn had Lisa been home with her in Connecticut.

Lisa's consciousness centered around her eyes. She never looked at herself, but was certain there was nothing there to see of herself but her consciousness. Her aunt, however, was in full view, body to toe, but the conversation was all telepathic.

The next thing she knew, they were at a street somewhere where the homes were contemporary and the sun was shining very brightly. She sensed joy and harmony just by walking with her aunt down the street. Her aunt gestured toward a home that was midsize and modern, with large contemporary windows in a style she'd seen in *Architectural Digest*. She found herself entering the home after absently walking past a closed garage door with two white Beetles parked side by side.

Inside, a large foyer with high ceilings opened up to skylights. She heard and smelled water, and to her right was a built-in waterfall cascading down to a large rectangular planter, which circulated the water. Plants hung from the edges of the planter and some from the ceiling. It was a stunning entrance.

She recalled glancing at her aunt, who beamed back, encouraging her to keep walking. She entered the foyer, and on her left was a large and airy living area full of cushioned seats in a fusion of bright colors, mostly blue with touches of white and yellow. It was serene and imbued her with a sense of hope. In the center of this huge living area, a pale-colored oriental rug held a glass table and chair.

On the chair sat her father, Ernest, typing away. Lisa stopped, stunned, as the man turned to smile radiantly back at his only daughter. Lisa could not believe her eyes. She knew she was dreaming, but the house felt so real and so did the feel of the carpet under her feet as she ran to meet him in a hug that would have broken her into tears had she been capable of it.

Through telepathy, he indicated he continued writing and inspired others on earth to write. That he, in fact, was "taking a break" from incarnations after the very traumatic life he'd had where his soul was almost taken. He read her thoughts and consoled her that he knew what effect he'd had on her life by being absent in a mortal body. However, he was there for her and would be watching her for the remainder of her current lifetime.

Ernest gave Lisa a tour of the house, completely forgetting about her aunt. They ended the tour by the two cars, and Lisa asked her father who had the second vehicle, which was identical to the Beetle her mother drove in her current lifetime. Ernest told her that her mother was well, would live a long life, but she would later join him in the house and drive the second car. Lisa recalled laughing, thinking that cars should not be a necessity in that dimension. Ernest only smiled in return and indicated that whatever made people more comfortable, they could create for their amusement. "Even ice cream," he indicated.

Lisa was given directions to her aunt's "house", which confused her, but as she waved goodbye to her father, she saw a street that looked vaguely familiar. As she walked down, she noted a Tudor-style home set away from the street. She found herself entering after hearing laughter through the open windows, a particular voice that reminded her of her grandmother's cheer when she'd regaled her with stories.

She entered. This house was different. It was austere with paneling, but very bright as well. Inside, she saw her aunt in the kitchen with her grandmother Adelaida, whom she had not seen since the previous summer when she visited. Her grandmother smiled, jovially asking her to join them in the kitchen, as they were preparing for a large party. Sonya explained to her that she would be living in the house "soon" and that she would be traveling with her "soon". Lisa was perplexed, but interpreted it as her aunt's desire in waking life to own her own home in the style of the house.

Lisa awakened to her alarm, the window still open to the breeze. As she went through her classes and sat with friends through lunch, she thought about her long vivid dream. Later in the day, her mother called to let her know her aunt Sonya had cancer.

Lisa sat in the library as she realized what her aunt in the dream had meant, and began to worry. Soon, her dreams would again take a different turn as graduation neared.

16. JOURNEYS WITH A DECEASED AUNT

Three weeks before graduation, Lisa's courses ended with final exams, then a week of activities acknowledging senior week. With pressures off from their rigorous courses, Lisa and her roommate, who'd both relocated to the upperclassmen dorms at the beginning of their junior year, joined their friends in a final week of outings and parties. Now returning after a late night of partying on the town's beach nearby, Lisa and her roommate gratefully crashed into their dorm and retired for the night. Unlike the other students, neither drank, but they were exhausted from the lateness of the hour. The suite, composed of a large room with two sofa beds, a small kitchen, dressing area and an adjoining private bath, was sequestered in a very quiet area of the campus.

Lisa loved the area with the surrounding neighborhood of fieldstone homes and manicured lawns. It provided a respite from the chaos of suburban New Haven and the mayhem that had not quieted since her aunt progressed to the terminal stage of her cancer. Fraught with grief, helpless to assist her aunt in her pain, Lisa was very troubled by the catastrophic illness and her mother's inability to process her own stress. Lisa was glad that before finals, her aunt had finally lapsed into a coma, where she no longer felt pain.

Lisa chose to avoid the situation by attempting to engross herself in her studies, but the impending death loomed like a dark shadow over her efforts to end her college years with success. Her energies divided by the issues at home, she continued with exams and passed, but without the honors she'd received while in high school.

Now done with what she felt was her best, she retired for the night, anticipating the rest of the "fun" week before the graduation ceremony. She lay down on the bed, turned her head toward her slumbering roommate across the way, and reveled in the quiet and restful sounds of the night.

Around 3 a.m. Lisa awakened from a dead sleep to see at the foot of her bed, a woman in a long black cloak with a hood over her head. It was her aunt. Sorrow marred Sonya's face, a fathomless sinking feeling causing Lisa's gut to turn. She sat up and glanced at the clock, unsure of whether it was one of her dreams. The vision faded, but the feeling of loss and profound loneliness remained.

That morning, Lisa recalled the vision vividly and told her roommate. She counseled her to call to see how she was at the hospital. Reluctantly, Lisa picked up their phone and dialed the hospital directly, knowing her mother or a family friend would have called if something had happened. The nurse told her her aunt was still in a coma. Lisa dressed, summoned her friend who had a car, and they visited. Uncle Roberto had flown overseas to be by his sister's bedside. He was there, and the look on his face told her everything.

Sonya passed a week before Lisa's graduation, exactly three nights to the hour when Sonya had visited Lisa in her dorm. She had gone to see Lisa to tell her she wouldn't make it to her college graduation after all. However, after all the arrangements were made, the wake and funeral over, and Roberto had flown back to rejoin their mother in San Juan, Sonya would return, as she'd promised to show her niece that life was full beyond the grave.

Summer came, and Lisa was back living with her mother, who had now purchased a home with her best friend. In the style of New Haven, homes in the '40s and '50s had three floors – each floor was large and separate, as they were intended to accommodate an entire family. Neala and her friend Lynda bought one of these older three-family homes. Lynda picked the first floor, which had a large porch in front, where her elderly mother sat on cool days to watch neighbors pass by. Neala and Lisa occupied the second floor, which also had three bedrooms and a porch right above Lynda's. The third floor was prepared for tenants, whose rent would help with Neala and Lynda's house repairs.

Lisa's bedroom faced the backyard, from where the detached two-car garage could be seen and the small garden adjacent to it. Two months after Sonya's death, Lisa had just retired in her new bedroom when she smelled the scent of Lily of the Valley, her favorite aunt's perfume. She didn't make the connection, but the scent calmed her so much that she fell promptly to sleep. Then, suddenly, like the evening in her single dorm room, she found herself sitting on a cement planter on the side of a sunny street – the message given to her telepathically was that she was in San Francisco.

Passersby came and went. As she turned her head to look down the street, she saw the ground angle down sharply. She was on a hill. A streetcar rolled at the lower end of the street at an intersection. Enthralled to find herself at a location she always wanted to see, she eagerly inclined her head and made to stand and walk about. She heard a woman's chuckle and looked to her right. Next to her sitting on the ledge, still chuckling, was her aunt Sonya. Sonya stood, and Lisa embraced her.

Rosy-cheeked, robust and full of vigor, Lisa was overjoyed at the way her aunt looked. Sonya introduced her to her "boyfriend": a man about her age who had "left" about six months before her own death. Suddenly, Lisa realized it was a dream. However, her aunt "told" her it was a "visit", not a dream: That now they would go to all the places they hadn't seen but planned on doing, unfettered by responsibilities, financial burdens or ill health – That they would now catch up on all those trips they couldn't take when the responsibilities of life took over.

The following night, the "visit" continued: different cities in the south, then Hawaii, where Lisa flew over the mouth of a volcano, then finally different locales in Europe. Sonya told her she planned on returning, but not for a while. She told Lisa she was always welcome to come along – to pray first, then ask for her – and she would come "running".

A few years passed. Then it was 1985.

Lisa visited California to see her uncle Roberto and his new wife, Marianne. It would become for her an annual visit, some-times biannual, as they revived their close relationship, akin to father and daughter. Lisa enjoyed the energy and openness of Los Angeles, the cuisine, so exciting and varied – the area so culturally diverse and accepting. She sought to find a position there and would live with her uncle and aunt until she could afford her own apartment.

One night, a "visit" resumed with her aunt Sonya after a period of silence. Lisa found herself joining her aunt at a large long table with a formal setting for several people. It had an atmosphere that was festive, replete with various dishes, desserts and women chatting merrily. They were all dressed in white, Lisa noticed. So was she. Sonya sat across from her, carrying hot dishes of food she had lovingly prepared. Seated, she was introduced to the women around the table. Food was passed, and the party was full of banter and the exchange of news.

Lisa relished her aunt's cooking. In life, Sonya loved to cook, experimenting on new dishes as her cookbook, left unpublished, attested. Now, she feasted on dishes she had not tasted since her hasty departure from San Juan. Though her grandmother excelled in cooking the traditional everyday dishes meant for ordinary mealtimes, her aunt Sonya mastered with flourish the complex dishes that were meant for large fiestas and parties. Sonya's love of cooking transcended death. There, spread out for all the guests and friends, were the dishes that were her halcyon.

Towards the end of the meal, dessert was brought to the table, then coffee and tea. It was then that the topic of who was new to the table arose. All the women turned to Lisa, welcoming her and asking questions. Lisa vaguely recalled telling them where she currently lived and her desire to procure work in California. The women, confused, turned to Sonya. Sheepishly, Sonya replied that Lisa was "returning". "Oh?" one said. Sonya explained she (Lisa) was just "visiting" since she missed her and the fiesta had the dishes she missed. A collective gasp issued from some of the women's lips.

"She's not supposed to be here," someone said. "She's not supposed to know what it's like here."

Sonya glanced guiltily at Lisa and then told the women she would make her promise "not to tell" what she had experienced. The women indicated Lisa would probably not remember upon returning to wakefulness. However, Lisa could not visit them again and partake of the food. Sonya looked at Lisa knowingly and winked. A week later, Lisa got a job interview. That night, Lisa was at Sonya's Tudor-style house to tell her the good news.

Sonya did not take her to see the other women again, but Lisa kept visiting.

Years later, Adelaida followed her daughter at a ripe old age of ninety-two. Lisa, still overseas in a job that didn't allow her to fly out to Manila for the funeral, missed her own beloved grand-mother's final days. This time, when Lisa "visited", Adelaida was now there in Sonya's living room, reunited with Roberto Sr., who had passed a few years before. Lisa also noted that her father was a regular visitor and so were her paternal grandparents.

In her "visits", parties happened often at Sonya's house. It seemed everyone got along in the afterlife. Shortly, however, upon her move to Pennsylvania years later to accept a contracted job, she noted her father was no longer around when she "visit-ed". As the visits in her "dreams" became less often, a new devel-opment in her waking life while living in Pennsylvania took place.

17. A SPIRITUAL AWAKENING

I solated in a new state from family and friends, Lisa spent an entire year acclimating to the new atmosphere of a subrural area with its forests, wildlife and the exclusive neighborhood of the "Main Line" nearby. Her internship job as a residential rehabilitation counselor paid little, but it was a stepping-stone to a hopefully more stable career in mental health care. Lisa loved the atmosphere of the rustic little towns, whose convenient access to the local commuter train was similar to the neighborhood where she'd attended university while living in Connecticut.

But the similarity ended there. The state was even more "conservative" and not as collegial or cosmopolitan as New Haven. The local area boasted some small colleges, which provided some stimulation, but still lacked the character of a university town steeped in tradition and openness to foreign influence.

Sequestered in a job with rotating hours, Lisa's sleep was interrupted by the changes in her internal clock, forced by the job, which demanded a change of shifts every few months. No dreams came. The following years provided more stability in hours, but her marriage precipitated several residential moves, and finally, a major illness, which almost took her life, revealed itself.

Lisa married a man who changed careers every year. The shift in income came with a change of location within the large state and, along with it, the chaos of stress that usually follows with every residential move. Lisa's health faltered after the fourth move in four years, revealing itself in a malignant lump nestled in her trachea, compromising her breathing.

As health care was tied to her job, the changes that came from lack of continuity as a school substitute took its toll. When Lisa finally settled down with a highly respected endocrinologist, he sent her for tests, which revealed what he dreaded: thyroid cancer, type 3. The ultrasound revealed it had spread to her sternum in her chest, from the large malignancy in her throat. With the news, family and friends from overseas and from her teen home in Connecticut prayed, said novenas, and requested masses on her behalf. Lisa, unable to fathom the catastrophe, turned to her Catholic upbringing and reached out from her lukewarm knowledge of prayer to praying fervently in her quest for wellness. Still in deep belief of the continuity of life after death, she reached out to her grandmother and her aunt Sonya from beyond the grave and connected them to her prayer requests with great urgency.

In the eighteen months of her recovery, Lisa discovered to her profound surprise and growing wellness that prayer was so powerful, and her faith became strong beyond measure. It was finally one night where she saw with her own eyes and ears the depth of the forces between good and evil.

As day settled into dusk, Lisa's then-husband came home from work and assisted her after her second and longest operation of seven and a half hours to make dinner. Weary from the anesthesia after just a few days from discharge, Lisa was resigned to preparing a simple meal for the couple. They had just overcome another major operation together, and Lisa could see that the stress of her illness was taking a toll on the marriage. Her husband had begun to smoke again.

Unable to deal with a confrontation about his health, Lisa quietly allowed the meal to progress and had retired early to bed at 8 p.m. when the sun had set. Her husband stayed downstairs in their two-bedroom townhouse, which had a large patio off of the living room. While he sat there watching TV, a breeze and then a wind had developed, and she shut the sliding glass door that led to the patio. Above him, Lisa dozed with the window open right above the patio door.

As Lisa began to doze, she was startled back to wakefulness when the crickets from the open window suddenly ceased. Normally, she would hear frogs as well from the nearby neighborhood swimming pool near their patio. Like a switch, silence descended into the room, and a sense of coldness pervaded and permeated the once-peaceful atmosphere. She felt someone or "something" staring at her from the window, where a breeze issued forth. Reluctantly, Lisa felt a once-familiar sense of dread, which she had experienced repeatedly at her grandmother's home in San Juan and as a toddler in Little Baguio.

She turned to look and saw a shadow of a man floating with a cape, darker than the night behind him. It seemed to hover in place, completely stationary dead center a few inches from the window. Aghast, Lisa knew it was a specter. It was completely in silhouette and exuded menace.

Determined to end the ghastly specter's visit, Lisa darted downstairs and opened the sliding glass door with vehemence, right under the window. Undaunted, she pulled out her rosary and the small bottle of holy water and started saying the "Our Father" out loud, sprinkling water at the area as she prayed. Her then-husband, a lukewarm Catholic, watched in awe and started mumbling a prayer with her, convinced there was something outside that had precipitated her exit from the warm bed in the room upstairs.

She looked up at the window. Nothing was there, but she continued praying. Moments later, the sense of dread disappeared, and she once again heard the chorus of cicadas and frogs from the nearby pool. She told her then-husband of the specter at the window, and he indicated that he had wondered why the television was "blinking" on and off during the time of her sighting. He indicated he felt like someone was looking in from the patio, but kept watching the television, convinced it might have been a curious neighbor or two passing by on the way to the pool.

A few weeks later, Lisa's malevolent encounter would be replaced by a lightness and wellness to her being, with a final visit from a being that left both her and her family astounded. It would forever alter her faith, and she would count every day as a blessing.

With Lisa's third and final cancer operation to remove the healthy thyroid as a way to ameliorate the possibility of any tumor metastasizing to the other gland, Lisa began to have "apprehension dreams", which plagued her. She was fearful after her ordeal that the cancer would return and invade another part of her body or another area of her neck. The operations had left her with a permanent scar, which on cold months would leave her feeling like a steel vise was around her neck, suffocating her.

Days and nights went by as Lisa continued to pray for recovery, and her unsuspecting colleagues remarked on her penchant for turtlenecks even in warmer weather. Only the supportive principal knew what she had undergone and continued to encourage and praise her for her work. As time marched into spring, the first anniversary of her diagnosis, Lisa slept fitfully, awaiting the end of the school year. She hoped for a better summer punctuated by vacations instead of visits to the doctor and hospital.

Her wish for assurance was granted.

On the week of Lisa's first anniversary of diagnosis, Lisa went about her day. A typical Friday, the week ended with emergencies: Her students who had issues at home usually "unraveled" on Fridays, when the thought of going home to an unstable home environment made them "act out". From bullying, fights and insubordination, Lisa saw it all at the inner-city school. It made for a usually hectic day, punctuated by calls to parents on what to anticipate.

Exhausted, Lisa drove the one-hour drive back to her more serene town, a village at that time, thankful she was well and away from the chaos. The couple customarily went out to eat on Fridays, and this was no exception. They ate a simple meal and threw on a video once they got home to just kick back and relax.

Around 9 p.m., Lisa left her then-husband's side to retire, trudging up the stairs to their second-floor bedroom. As the temperature was still chilly on April nights, the windows remained closed near their bed. Apprehensively, Lisa clutched her rosary, the same one she had held on to since her first operation and insisted the nurse hang under her operating room table.

She dozed, clinging to the rosary, determined not to let it go because of the specter she had seen at the window. She dreamed. In the dream, it was the dead of night, as her husband was now asleep next to her. At the foot of the bed, she dimly saw a bright light issue from the open door from the hallway. Curious, she focused on the light, which became more pronounced as if something was coming into the room.

Lisa watched as the light entered the room. It did not hurt her eyes, so that she was able to see the light's origin: A man with a halo on his head, his face obscured by brilliance. No sound issued from the entrance, but the man approached her bedside and leaned over her face. She sensed a strong feeling of serenity and security that was so deep that she struggled to see the man who was by her side. She heard the man whisper a prayer in a language unfamiliar to her. As he prayed, he made the sign of the cross on her forehead, the rough texture of his cloak touching her cheek.

Lisa struggled to see the man whose benevolence overwhelmed her. She wanted to thank him. She attempted to look at his face, but was told in a voice in her head she was not "ready". She looked down, humbled by the voice, and saw that the man's feet were sandaled in some type of leather material. Recognition flooded her being as the man's hand took her own fingers and helped her wind the rosary around a button on her flannel gown.

With that being done, she sensed the light move away, and the man silently departed as quietly as he came. Lisa slept the sleep of a child in serenity and profound peace that she had not done since her diagnosis the year before.

Lisa awakened the next day, her then-husband already up and brewing coffee downstairs. She got up, recalling the dream vividly, and felt the peace steal within her. Feeling energized and in full wakefulness, she felt a weight lifted from her and a lightness she had not had in a long time.

Lisa approached the bathroom, thinking of her dream and its significance. As she did so, she glanced at the bathroom mirror and recoiled in surprise: There, on her chest, wound around a top button of her flannel nightgown, was her rosary.

18. STRANGE ROADS

With her divorce finalized, Lisa's life returned to stability, and it was in her new single life where she renewed her interests and caught up with her travels overseas. It was finally with a new job where Lisa was provided the much-needed respite from being a substitute on call. Still recovering from the unstable marriage she'd finally terminated after the tumultuous turn of her health, her outlook improved with the impetus provided by her encounter with the being of benevolence.

Hired into a permanent position, Lisa loved her job as a schoolteacher in a small but highly respected school district located near the Amish community. While there, she was highly respected and appreciated by her peers, her principals and the superintendent, who was well aware she was envied by some of her colleagues. Lisa made friends and, in the process, started to relax and pursue cultural events. But after three years of commuting an hour each way on the highway, it started to take a toll despite the joys of the career.

One early morning in the dead of winter, Lisa was driving in darkness, moving at about fifteen miles per hour on a very icy highway on her way to work. Ahead of her, an old late model car that looked vintage was gaining on her in the left lane. Lisa moved to the right lane when she realized she was no longer alone. The left lane seemed plowed and cleared, whereas the right lane had a sheen of black ice.

Gingerly, Lisa navigated the slick surface, her cell phone by her side for emergencies. The "vintage" car, something from the '50s, decided to overtake her, moving to her lane. Aggravated that the car seemed intent on either tailing her or moving in front, Lisa moved back to the left lane and overtook the car despite the road's slick surface. She didn't need to take a chance that the car might brake suddenly in front of her.

Ahead again by a few feet, Lisa moved back to the safety of the right lane, the car now behind her. She noted a third vehicle, a small truck carrying a load of hay. The truck looked very old and in poor shape. In her rearview mirror, she noted the truck was in the left lane she had just vacated and was now side by side with the vintage car as if in a race.

Lisa watched in horror as the truck made a maneuver to overtake the vintage car, changing lanes. The truck plowed into the car, turning over on top of the car in a flurry of snow. Lisa saw this all in her rearview mirror in what seemed like total silence as if in an old movie. There was absolutely no sound to the crash.

Suddenly, in a flash, she was several yards ahead. Though her foot had paused over the accelerator in those few seconds of shock while she watched, she was somehow half a football field away from the accident, which had just taken place before her startled eyes. Seeking to control her vehicle, which had somehow slid ahead by several yards, she reached for the phone on the seat. She dialed 911 and reported the whereabouts of the accident and gave her name. As she gave the description of both vehicles, she realized they were both very old.

Lisa wondered and told a friend at work about the incident. She could not fathom how she managed to be several yards away seconds before the accident, which could have involved her in the collision.

Two weeks later, on the way home from work, Lisa was about three miles from home and close to the exit where her town was located. The road was now clear, the ice and snow melted as the weather gave the area some respite from another snowfall. Lisa slowed to ease to the right lane and promptly fell asleep behind the wheel.

Suddenly, a large hand with a strong arm slammed on her steering wheel, moving the wheel back to the right lane. Lisa awakened to the loud sound in time to see the masculine hand and arm. She looked up in terror at the passenger seat, where she saw a man who was so tall that his shoulders went past the roof of the Jeep she was driving. Suddenly, she came to full wakefulness, realizing she had fallen asleep. As she grabbed the steering wheel, the strange hand from a few seconds ago disappeared in a flash.

Lisa was alone again. Shaken by the bizarre incident, she eased the Jeep over and exited the highway. Upon returning to her apartment, she parked, inspected the Jeep, and wondered who or what it was that saved her from an accident once again.

The third mishap involved a large doe, which crossed the same highway the next fall. Lisa decelerated in time before the animal would have crashed through the windshield. Seconds before impact, something shoved the animal so that it turned towards the guardrail, where it leaped over and stopped on the shoulder, watching.

The fourth and final accident was the major event that precipitated Lisa's decision to finally join her new husband, who lived two counties away. It was both a career move and a change of lifestyle, which enabled her a chance to investigate the paranormal.

On the evening of a program presentation at the high school where Lisa worked, she left for home to shower and change. She joined the traffic on her return drive, dressed and ready to eat dinner before the event. Lisa had been invited to join her friend Jane for dinner with her husband at their home, just minutes from the high school. She never made it there.

Again, it was the height of winter when Lisa stopped at a four-way intersection just minutes from her friends' home, where she was expected for dinner. To her right a large mound of snow obscured her vision of the oncoming traffic, her left, clear. She proceeded and noted an oncoming black van several yards from the intersection. Halfway through, she was stunned to find that it felt like a train had just come through and broadsided her.

Lisa came to a few seconds later to discover her Toyota Camry in the opposite lane, facing traffic. People gawked at her through their windshields as three green "balloons" popped out of her dashboard. She heard a distinct hissing sound above her and noted the entire windshield was a spider's web. On the passenger seat, her tire sat next to her, a testament to the strength of the impact. Then a dreaded popping and creaking sound awakened her to the reality of the accident.

The hissing was from gas leaking out of the van's interior. As she looked up, she noted the van was sitting upside down on the roof of her car. The rest of the vehicle had imploded except for the bubble where she sat. Lisa quickly attempted to open the door to no avail. She reached for the window, but the automatic was off. She reached for a small screwdriver she kept handy for emergencies and pushed the sharp end to the middle of the window, now anxious to escape.

The window exploded in shards, and Lisa climbed out, head

first, now smelling the gas. She stumbled onto the pavement and darted headlong into the field of wheat ahead, heedless of the watching traffic, where a woman yelled for her to stop, as she might have injuries.

"Run! It's about to explode!" Lisa heard herself yell to the group of people with blankets ready to cover her. She leapt into the wheat and disappeared.

Minutes passed. Lisa jetted up to look at the van as it started to slide off her car. Then an ambulance and a police car with flashing lights started making its way toward the wreck.

A woman approached with a blanket, and Lisa finally joined her in her vehicle. She had no injuries visible to her, and as she sat in the back seat of the woman's car, the woman told her she was a nurse and introduced her daughter, who smiled graciously. Lisa watched as the police and the EMTs went to locate Lisa in her car, unable to find anyone. They then pulled the man from the van, who appeared injured. The men scattered, looking for Lisa, who sat in shock in the back of the vehicle.

"She's here! She's okay," the woman yelled, popping her head from her rolled-down window. A high school student Lisa recognized opened her door, checked her vital signs, and slid a pallet onto the seat. They asked her to lie on it, and she was pulled out. Lisa passed out, relieved she had been found.

She awakened to find herself lying on a gurney in the local emergency room. She listened to the murmurs of the "incredible accident", talking about her running for the field in front of everyone – "miraculously coming out of a car that was totally pancaked". *Surely, you jest,* Lisa thought. She felt around her body for pains and injuries, touched her head, opened and shut her eyes, and noted her sensitivity to the light above her. She dimly thought, *I have a concussion.*

She had a concussion. That was all she had. She awakened

in a private room, where a policeman smiled down at her. She asked how the other man was. "He's fine," he reassured her. Lisa sat up, realizing she had missed the school's presentation, where she was expected to talk. The man laughed and told her, "I don't think so."

It was morning.

Lisa was discharged the next day, and her boyfriend, William, came to pick her up and decided to see about her car. They went to where the car had been towed. Her fiancé could not believe his eyes. One of the staff at the towing service, unaware of who was the driver, started telling William how he felt so bad for the passenger of the vehicle. He hoped she was alive and was extending his condolences if not.

"She's here," William said, gesturing behind them towards Lisa.

The man turned in astonishment when he saw Lisa standing behind him. "How did you ever...!"

"I ran from the scene, thinking the gas was going to explode."

19. ABOARD A CRAFT

After the vehicle accidents and near-fatal accidents, Lisa finally moved a few counties to join William. She had to find another job, since the school, which she loved, was more than two hours' drive away. Her new home was close to several tourist spots, serenely tucked in a corner of the state where a creek ran a few yards from the property. In this enclave of homes, both silence and the beauty of nature reigned. Once she settled in, Lisa started to have very unusual dreams, which repeated over several months.

The main bedroom faced the backyard, which had a few birch trees, tall and full of foliage. Next to their home, another home sat half an acre away. A few yards from the neighbor's back door, a creek separated the homes from the woods beyond. The atmosphere was pastoral and quiet especially at night. In this setting, Lisa set up house, enjoying the space and privacy in which her three dogs could run.

One night in the fall, Lisa settled down early and prepared for bed. As it was early fall, she opened the bedroom windows to the cooling breeze and snuggled in. The windows in the room bracketed the bed in such a way that it was almost over their heads. In the middle of the night, still asleep, Lisa sensed a breeze from the window near her and made a move to close it. Still between sleep and wakefulness, she discovered in her disoriented state that she couldn't move.

She sensed a presence in the room, immediately to her right by the open window. Whatever it was prevented her from opening her eyes as she struggled to move an arm to protect herself. Whatever it was seemed to lean over and was examining her neck, the site of the thyroid cancer operation she'd had a few years before her divorce. She sensed something brush against her neck like a feather, then a face. Her anxiety ratcheted up, and finally breaking one arm free, she awakened.

The room was empty. Sleep paralysis?

A few nights later, the event repeated itself. This time, Lisa's arms would not move, and she started attempting to speak. Whatever it was seemed to be scrutinizing her neck, even gently poking her with what felt like puffs of air. Terrified, she told William the next morning. William told her one of the dogs surely would have awakened to the intrusion. He threw it up to a nightmare and her overactive imagination.

For several nights, Lisa would sleep only to come awake to a presence in the room. In each of the instances, she found she could not yell out, open her eyes, nor reach for her boyfriend to awaken him. After several episodes, whatever it was finally stopped when one night, Lisa broke free from the "grip" and succeeded in pinwheeling one arm free. She yelled, and she distinctly heard a "click" right next to her and a movement.

The room was empty when she finally opened her eyes.

In the coming days, Lisa would notice when she looked in the mirror that her scar from the thyroid operation had shrunk and seemed to be less noticeable. She also did not have feeling in that area of her neck all the way to her jaw. However, the feeling had fully returned that morning, and she was surprised how the nerves seemed to have regenerated almost overnight. She had had a series of major operations just five years ago to the day, and the nerves were repeatedly compromised from the major operations that took both her thyroids away. Perplexed but thankful, Lisa's spiritual side became more tuned to the benevolent God she so admired. She became even more religious and made prayer, now a ritual, a part of her day ever since the "visitation" and the rapid recovery from the cancer. This was a cancer that had been x-rayed and documented to have spread to her lungs by a major university hospital. After that visitation from the man in light in her bedroom, a later X-ray just two weeks later showed no spots in her lungs.

As winter took hold of the region, snow became a daily chore, which made travel once again a touch-and-go affair. No longer tasked with navigating a highway, but a slower two-lane blacktop, Lisa's commute to work became less of a challenge. That solved, her energies turned to her new surroundings and the charming town that was just a few miles from her doorstep. Routine brought peace. Shortly, while sharing coffee with a friend from work one morning, the woman noticed Lisa was limping after a jog. The lady introduced her to one of the area's coveted treasures: a chiropractor and natural healer who had a gift of healing. Shortly, Lisa met with the chiropractor, who seemed very spiritually tuned to the biological energies of her clients. Lisa sensed the woman's distinctiveness and reveled in finding her. For her, the woman was another blessing sent her way.

A few weeks into her back treatment, where she learned her scoliosis had come back, Lisa was running again, no longer in need of orthopedic inserts and the possibility of back surgery. Her disenchantment with the medical establishment became complete. As her health progressed, losing weight by a regimen of repeat detoxifications, Lisa became buoyant and "was getting

younger" by the minute, so friends concluded, and "may disappear if she turned sideways" and was "wired to dance" according
to her humorous colleagues in the office.

It was during this time that Lisa's dreams, dormant for a
while, started to introduce her to something different. A few
weeks after her final twenty-one-day cleanse guided by the
chiropractor, who was a naturopath, Lisa's energies were high as
her body bounced back from the toxins and the depletion from
cancer years ago. She changed her diet to almost vegan, her
daily regimen mostly raw organic vegetables and fruits. She felt
a "keenness" to her senses, even her eyesight, as she'd always
had myopia. For a period of time, she was driving without her
glasses.

One early Friday evening, Lisa went to bed earlier than usual
after a taxing week at work. William was watching TV as usual
and decided to stay until the 11 p.m. news. Lisa settled down with
a book, a war novel about the holocaust. Troubled by the images
from the book she was reading, she finished her evening by
praying, surrounded by her rosary and prayer books.

She "awakened" vividly surrounded by white light. This
time, unlike the dreams where she felt unable to move or speak,
she felt she was standing in a large room with several "people".
Lisa looked around her, the sounds, the images, so clear. The
"people" were all dressed in white just like the room, whose
source of light seemed to emanate from the entire ceiling. There
was some type of serene music like that from a flute in the background. She felt very happy, almost unfettered and free from
any problems. The people in white robes exuded benevolence,
deep love and peace.

She felt very drawn to them as they telepathically conversed
with her, telling her she had now approached a different "gal-
axy" – that they were now right outside a different "place". A
bald older man in white robes, taller than the rest, invited her to

come to the "window" on the side of the room, which seemed round. The window was convex, jutting out so that it was like the side of a fishbowl. Lisa was invited to sit on the edge or even recline and relax if she wished.

Lisa eagerly climbed on the window like she had as a child in her grandmother's house. She reclined on the glass, totally relaxed, and looked out. She was rewarded with a scene she told herself she needed to embed in her memory, as the sight was so beautiful.

The view was 180 degrees: Different types of "ships" of varying sizes and colors she had never seen in waking life passed by and paused at the window. She got the impression they were passing to show her what she had always wanted to see or was waiting to see. Enchanted, she watched them fly by a background of a city with spires. Despite the city's size, the sky was clean, ethereal and filled with a "light" she could not comprehend. There was no glare or harshness as she beheld the vast city and beautiful and enthralling ships that flew effortlessly past her window.

Some of the craft felt "alive" as they spiraled with gossamer tails; some were like an opening fan, closing again as they flew past. Some were so large that they covered the entire span of the window, and she could see "people" waving at her from their windows as the ship went past.

The ships' flights were so fluid and graceful. They flew like they were sentient beings, like birds that could swiftly turn on a dime – and some of them did. The bald man seemed to be communicating with the ships outside, as when she "heard" his request for the ship to turn or pause for Lisa to see them better, they did. One glimmered with what seemed like translucence within which there were several pastel-colored lights. Another had a beautiful gossamer tail like a peacock, swooshing in silence and pausing for her to see. Another was like a long rocket, which when it stopped in midair, blossomed into a flower, then, finally, into the shape of two plates put together.

Another huge vehicle encompassed the breadth of the window with its lights gleaming from within its body – two halves of a plate with light blue and green alternating, like marble. They were all so silent, and she sensed a festive atmosphere from them like a parade.

Lisa turned to the man in white and asked where they were going. He "told" her they were all engaged in some type of "commerce": some had a "mission" to bring back something, some were visiting neighbors who were far away (carrying passengers), and some needed to barter "goods". He told her that everyone was part of a large "community", where each planet had a role and a desire to be part of a greater good. That "they", including the people in the room, were all part of a membership of planets and neighboring galaxies.

Lisa asked him about Earth. He told her that "they" too someday will be part of this "cooperation". But no, Earth was not part of them. It was by itself at this time. There was an element of sadness and disappointment in the man when the topic was discussed. The instant replay in her head that came was that the Earth was in a dense state that required much development.

Earth was being isolated, therefore, as it was "not prepared" for a certain kind of "light". Earth was competitive, not cooperative, angry and not at peace. As a planet, Earth's beings were of a vibration that was imperfect, dense, malignant. That few on Earth felt it was a duty to help, to love and to be patient. That Earth souls had a penchant for destroying the planet because of selfish pursuits.

The man told Lisa that all pursuits that were worthwhile had to do with creation, invention, serenity and well-being. That the animals on the planet were there to balance the soul of man to teach him lessons – lessons that he is unable to learn. As the man kept speaking, Lisa was distracted by the constant beauty around her, the sense of peace and enveloping love. She wanted to stay, but was told her time was up. She was told she had to earn the feeling of constant joy, which was the state she would find herself in if she were to stay.

Lisa was unclear whether she was witnessing "heaven", where her aunt and grandmother were, including the father she missed. She did not recall a response nor did she recall where she was in the universe.

She awakened to Saturday, wondering about the nature of the "dreams". Little did she know, she was about to get her answer.

20. THE MICHELIN MAN VISITATIONS

L isa would visit the "room" again, where she was introduced to some of the beings she encountered on the first "visitation". In the final analysis, she concluded everyone there had a function, and the relationships were devoid of conflict or interpersonal problems. Everyone, despite the number of beings she met, got along, respected each other, and were content.

Eventually she met beings that looked drastically different from her, but despite the differences in physique, it did not lead to prejudice or discrimination of certain groups. There was a sense of "fun" among the beings and a shared sense of purpose she had not observed in human beings as much when there was diversity.

There were beings who were short and had elongated heads with very little hair. There were exceptionally willowy beings who radiated light from within, and then there were ones that could only be felt, but not seen. When she was in the "ship" but not in "Earth" reality, according to the old man in white, she could communicate with all of them. It was a lesson on the limits of three-dimensionality. Those who were ethereal were spiritually very refined – thus they were more attuned to a creator she understood could only be seen by very few.

Several, she was told, were in the room with her, but she, even in her ethereal state, would not be able to see them, as she still needed to "vibrate" at a certain frequency in order to do so. Those beings with those high frequencies, she was told, were responsible for mending and recreating what man destroys on Earth – and were responsible for Lisa's feeling of well-being. The feeling of joy felt magnified because of their presence, though unseen, in the room. By being in their presence, she was told, she was constantly being "healed" in spirit.

Lisa awakened from that long dream feeling a sense of profound peace and almost like an epiphany. Then a period of silence. Lisa took this respite to retell her dreams to her chiropractor, whom she respected and admired. It wasn't so much the dream itself she recounted, as what insight she'd derived from the encounter about metaphysics. Lisa saw the "dreams" as her own success at astral projection. It was God's answer to a plea to have an out-of-body experience, which she had been attempting since she was a young teen.

As work became routine, Lisa kept separate her enriched private life learning about the nature of reality in the cosmos. She became very eager to seek people in real time who might share her desire to "see" at night while in a dream state. Lisa and William started looking forward to more vacations overseas and would begin traveling with tours and, finally, independently every summer. The trips would open Lisa to a keener awareness of how prevalent abroad the paranormal events were encountered by people, but closer to home, she would once again be visited by the unexpected as she sent out her desire for more knowledge to the universe.

On a spring evening in 2002, as Lisa was getting ready for the summer and a long-anticipated trip to Spain, Lisa was packing late into the night. As the couple retired to bed, Lisa decided to open the window to the warming breeze in the extra bedroom where the dogs slept and where the luggage lay open nearby.

A strong wind blew in, slamming the door behind her. She turned in time to hear the unmistakable "snap" and "hum" that seem to accompany an interesting night of dreams. She opened the door, shut it behind her, and crossed to their bedroom. She kept that door open as she settled under the covers, the breeze from their own window blowing through into the hallway. Lisa must have instantly fallen asleep, as the first thing she was aware of was her body once again flying through space just like the first time she'd "voyaged" with her aunt.

With great anticipation, Lisa expected her "trips" with her aunt Sonya to recommence, but she remained alone as she "flew" from one spot to another. She sensed somehow she was near the vicinity of her house. Then, below her, a forest opened up. She felt herself almost descend, then she saw an opening – a lake below her. Still fearful of drowning, Lisa instinctively cringed at the thought of meeting the water. Then she sensed a calm overtake her, and she turned to her right. Flying next to her was a man covered in a white suit from head to toe. The only way she can describe it is he was like the Michelin Man in the tire commercial on TV. She got an unmistakably strong impression she'd known him since the beginning of time.

The man communicated telepathically and vibrated a very strong sense of love and kindness. She was overwhelmed by the feeling of benevolence and felt she was safe with this very familiar being. As soon as Lisa became better acclimated to their speed of flight and had calmed, she "awakened" to find herself in her father's "neighborhood", where her aunt had shown her his "home".

The Michelin Man stood next to her and seemed to be communicating that he and her father were one. Lisa became confused and did not understand. The man took her by the hand and led her down the neighborhood, and she got the message "In my house there are many mansions..." She found it familiar, then realized it was directly quoted from the Bible itself.

Pointedly, she thought, "What does that mean?"

The man communicated that she was asking what she already knew in her being. Reincarnation. Like she learned in the books she had read as an adolescent: Lobsang Rampa, the Seth books, Gina Cerminara and others. As they moved through the streets, she saw people. All seemed in a state of happiness. Most, if not all, were laughing in the company of each other, strolling in a park or seen through open windows of their perfect houses.

"How were they built?" she asked in her head.

He replied in his head, "By thought, just like creation."

Suddenly, Lisa found herself bodily being hugged face-to-face by the Michelin Man as she descended from the ceiling of her bedroom. He was dropping her down gracefully back on her side of the bed, his face radiant, inches from her own. She sensed panic, a desire not to be back – to stay with him. He gently told her it wasn't time. Someday.

Lisa awakened as soon as she felt her consciousness reenter her solid body to find a dark and empty ceiling. Her ears clicked, and a "snap" came from within her head.

She was back.

In the weeks that followed, Lisa would meet one of William's friends, a man named "Jack" (pseudonym), who was in training to become a field investigator for a local UFO organization. She became very intrigued and in short order had signed up to receive the training manual. She started studying to become one. It was 2008, just a few months from the beginning of a UFO flap in Pennsylvania.

By mid-March, Lisa had passed the field investigator test in one sitting and was introduced to the local investigative group, which only had two others. One left shortly after their first meeting, and she was assigned her first cases immediately. This involvement with the volunteer organization dedicated to alien discovery would lead her to some of the most bizarre and enlightening cases of her personal career. Shortly, she discovered the prevalence of witnesses just within her county.

21. THREE DISPATCH REPORTS

From the beginning of April to the end of November, Lisa was involved in assisting with witness reports, which came through the volunteer organization's website. Unable to navigate the extensive area of the county, she contacted far-off witnesses by phone and recorded their statements on the investigators' portal. It was a UFO flap, which ended up on a map she created with tacks, showing the preponderance of sightings within her county for the benefit of the state director and a film crew enlisted by the MUFON chairman.

During this time, Lisa had the opportunity to become involved in an episode for TV about the flap, which aired for the first time during Thanksgiving. It was shortly after this that locals identified her on the street and began approaching her with their own stories, confident they would not be ridiculed. However, despite Lisa's reassurances, the witnesses who spoke with her in person would not divulge their names nor divulge those who witnessed the events with them. One of them had taped the sighting from their vehicle while the car rolled down the highway, but would not share the video even after Lisa drove to meet with them at a diner an hour away.

The following year Lisa was recruited to become part of a dispatch team, which became a frustrating endeavor. Lisa discovered that this team was funded primarily to seek alien technology. Reports that came "hot" from the witness reporting website that alluded to or appeared to entail an alien abduction were not taken as seriously as those with craft technology. Lisa's training as a mental health counselor and interviewer helped her lend an empathetic ear to the distressed experiencers, but not to obtain information on saucer characteristics or the technology involved.

Disenchanted and disappointed, Lisa's interest waned and so did her attendance at the meetings online, which came on short notice, compromising her concentration at work the next day. She left the organization and sought others whose interests were not political or for self-gain, but rather to discover the reason for the human abductions and animal mutilations.

As a final gesture to the organization, she organized a UFO conference on behalf of the director and during that conference found out about author Dolores Cannon. She would not forget the witnesses she interviewed after reading Cannon's numerous books, which resonated with her due to their spiritual and metaphysical quality.

One of the cases that came Lisa's way while "on call" on the dispatch site (a four-hour stint where she would receive an online witness report and was required to call the witness within the hour to determine if field agents should be dispatched by the director) came from a woman she will call "Sally". Sally's distressed report came through at the beginning of a shift, and Lisa, alarmed for the woman's safety, called her immediately at the given number. The location has been changed to keep the woman anonymous:

"Sally" lived in a large five-bedroom home located at the fringes of a large wooded area near the Canadian border. Due to her husband's line of work, she was left home alone most of the time. Her children, now grown with families of their own, would visit from other parts of the region.

On this one particular evening, Sally was once again alone in the large house. She had been watching TV after dinner, but decided to retire to bed and read a new book. As she prepared for bed, she noted through the open window of her bedroom, which overlooked a field and the woods beyond, a red light in the distance. It was just barely above the tree line, but still very visible because of its odd red color. Sally ignored it and sat in bed, reading her book. A few minutes later, she was distracted from reading by a light at the corner of her eye.

Sally looked to her left, where the window was located. She noticed that the red light, which was only a pinprick the first time she had seen it minutes before, was now the size of a dime. Intrigued, she got up and approached the window, which was shut against the cold chill.

The light was round and seemed to be a fiery red ball. With alarm, she noticed it approach her house, passing over the woods. She now knew it wasn't the setting sun, as she had thought before. As it skimmed over the field ahead of her, Sally pulled the shades down and drew the curtains. She leaped back into bed, covering herself with the blankets as if for protection.

Then she got up and bolted down the steps in her slippers to check the doors to the front and back of the house. She distinctly recalled they were bolted and locked, as she was always alone and had been reminded several times over the years to bolt them. She distinctly recalled returning up the stairs when the lights in her bedroom started to buzz and blink.

Sally leaped for the bed and shut the lamps off as if to obscure her location from whatever lay beyond the window. The next thing Sally would remember was she was lying with the covers completely off her body. She was flat on her back, and something terrifying was staring down at her. It appeared to be a large insect, the eyes huge and multifaceted like a mosquito's. Paralyzed and unable to scream, Sally watched in horror as the creature reached towards her lower abdomen with its wiry legs. All about it suggested a human-size insect of some type. The creature was silent and devoid of feeling. It did not react to her fear, but seemed to ignore her like one would an experimenter towards a lab animal.

The creature extended some type of long object made of metal, and it inserted it through Sally's navel. Sally felt her uterus being manipulated like an examination through the device. Then the creature was gone.

Now able to move, Sally got up, convinced she had been awake through the entire episode. She reached for her phone, noticing it was past midnight. She called her son, who was several miles away. He told her to check the doors and to call the police if something was amiss. Hanging up, she checked the window and noticed the red ball receding towards the woods in a matter of minutes.

She bolted for her lamp, turned it on, and checked her navel. She had a red welt right in it, but it didn't hurt or feel tender. Now convinced something had happened, she ran back down the steps, afraid of what might still be in the house. She turned the lights on as she went, but nothing had moved, and the doors were still locked, as she had left them.

Sally spoke with her son, who arrived in the morning at first light, recounting her "nightmare". She showed him the welt that was still visible on her navel. To allay her fears, he told her to see a doctor. The following week, a doctor saw her and referred her to a specialist.

Sally spoke with Lisa again two weeks later. She had filed a report on the same site, now reporting more of the encounter. When Lisa called her, the same frightened woman was now even more alarmed: she had been diagnosed with uterine cancer. Her question was: Did the creature know about her cancer and was trying to alert her? Or did the creature introduce something into her body that created the cancer? We will never know.

Another case involved a prominent figure who lived on a ranch in the Midwest. For the purposes of anonymity, the gentleman's name has been changed. "Joe" and his son live on a large hundred-acre livestock farm. One night right after a late dinner, Joe and his family overheard a commotion in one of the barns where the cows were housed.

Concerned with wildlife in the vicinity, Joe leaped into his truck, accompanied by his oldest son, to check. They each carried a rifle and flashlights, as the pasture was pitch dark at that late hour.

As the truck approached the largest barn, they saw a whirling blue light, bright like a neon sign, but spinning vertically like a large spiral lollipop right behind the roof. Joe reported that there was little sound, so it wasn't a conventional craft with spotlights, as he'd previously surmised. However, a low whirring sound was palpable.

They could hear the cows inside the barn. Now leaning against the barn's wall, Joe approached in stealth, trying to determine the source of the whirling blue light. It was now over the roof, and the cows were increasingly agitated. He entered the barn, shutting the door behind him. He could see some of the light through holes in the roof, but except for a mist over the ceiling of the barn itself, he found nothing. He shut the door securely and bolted for the truck to report the strange incident.

The following night, the report came through again. The whirling blue light, larger than ever, had returned. A group of field agents were dispatched to the scene to determine the nature of the anomaly. The anomaly appeared interested in the cattle, as once again it was seen at the vicinity of the barn where these cows were housed.

A third interesting case comes closer to home, where a woman within the county where Lisa resided was driving home from her choir practice on a busy route. "Cindy" was a young newlywed, who kept in touch with her mother by joining her every Tuesday evening for choir practice at her mother's local church, a county away. One evening, en route to the church, she distinctly felt she was being followed.

The highway Cindy takes is a relatively busy road, especially at that hour, as traffic does not abate on that highway until close to 7 p.m. She looked at her rearview mirror at the traffic, to her right and finally to her left outside her windshield to find that there were a series of lights following her. She thought nothing of it until at the conclusion of choir practice she was driving on the same route home and found the same series of lights following her as she headed in the opposite direction. By then it was close to 9 p.m., and the traffic was lighter. The lights followed her until she exited onto the road leading to her street.

Cindy met with Lisa at a local diner to show her the video of the lights, which her husband took. After repeated occurrences, she was spooked, and he rode shotgun to tape the event. A row of five to six white lights about five hundred feet to the left of the car showed on the video. They did not appear attached to a larger structure, as they moved independently and at times moved closer to the viewer than others.

At that meeting, Cindy disclosed that what ultimately led them to decide to report it was how the lights at the last choir practice followed her all the way home. As she coasted the last few miles to her street, she saw to her horror that between the trees, she saw the series of lights still following her. As she rolled her car into the garage, she shut the garage door and ran in, locking all the doors. When she looked out her kitchen window, the lights were now stationary and hovering over the house, as if waiting.

Reports such as these are frustrating, since there was self-reported corroborative evidence (the spouse who filmed the lights) and, if the video can be trusted, a video of the event. However, for some reason that will probably never be known, the witness and her spouse never relinquished a copy of the video she showed Lisa that evening. The witness promised she would upload the video and attach it in an email and include it in their report, but neither an email to Lisa or an upload of the video was made to the reporting site.

As the flap abated, the show on UFOs aired. It would lead to people approaching Lisa with stories they refused to report on the website, choosing once again to remain unnamed. This time, the witnesses were up close, and the terror and confusion was personal.

W hile exiting a store one afternoon, Lisa was approached by a man who recognized her from the show she was involved in. Eager to tell his unusual story, he asked that he and his girlfriend remain anonymous. A wooded area near the Delaware River has been the site of a few sightings and uncannily eerie events. Just along this river in Bucks County is a park situated in a less-traveled location despite its proximity to busy New Jersey. It was in this park that his girlfriend, whom we will call "Anne", found herself jogging alone.

The state park Anne frequents is a park longer than it is wide. It hosts large, high trees, which bend down to the river's edge, and has a path that leads from one end to the other. On lazy Sunday afternoons, teenagers and families can be found enjoying the outdoors, picnicking around the grassy area, taking in the scenery of the river and the narrow canal that lies adjacent.

Anne jogs every day and chose to jog after work on this particular day. The park closes at sunset, but on a late fall day, the sunset comes earlier than she would have wished. As she began her jog, the other people had left since the darkness made a rapid approach during that time of year. The park lends a sense of isolation with its large sheltering trees and bushes. This made the paths lonely and impenetrably dark even in early evening.

As Anne began her jog, she noticed that the cars in the parking lot she passed had departed. She spotted her car far off in the distance near the park's entrance and hoped that her last-minute hastily parked car on the side of the narrow road did not get hit as the cars attempted to pass. She decided to finish her jog despite the park's closing at dusk, as she was already there.

The park itself had a canal along one side of the Delaware – the side she was on. She decided to jog along the canal, then turn and head back at the end. A few miles later, she was jogging towards her car from the opposite direction and noticed a pair of lights coming toward the rear of her car.

Thinking it was a police car patrolling the area, she decided to make a run towards her car before it was ticketed. As she came closer, she realized that the two lights did not belong to a police cruiser, since they appeared to her now as a few feet higher than her car's roof. Attempting to shake a growing sense of unease, she bolted for the driver's side door, clicked it, and noted that whatever the light was issuing from was definitely something she had not seen before.

Anne recounted to her boyfriend that she distinctly remembered getting in the driver's seat, but for some reason, she felt compelled to come out again. She found herself standing right outside her open door, facing the back of the car. A creature had emerged from the direction of the two blinding lights, and when it was finally approaching her, her throat constricted in a scream. Bolted to the ground, she watched in terror as the creature came closer and stopped a few feet in front of her. It was about eight to nine feet tall and resembled a praying mantis.

The mantis extended a long insectoid arm and reached for Anne. The next thing she knew, she was again sitting in her driver's seat with the door closed. She looked down at her watch, and she noted with astonishment that it was morning. Her watched showed 6:30 a.m.

Anne's boyfriend recounted how she called him very shaken by the incident that morning. When he came to see her, she showed him small rounded depressions in even spaces going down one leg from her knee to right above her ankle. They were reportedly painless when touched and were not red or irritated. How she got them, no one knows.

A second incident reported by two men at a coffeehouse involves one late evening when two men, "Mike" and "Mark", were commuting together on their way home from work. Since they lived just minutes apart, they had decided to save on gas by carpooling every day to their job across the river in New Jersey.

On a winter evening, both men approached the Jersey side of a bridge, when they saw a dark-colored van stopped on the bridge. Mark, who was driving, asked his companion to step out and check after he noted that the van wasn't paused in traffic, but actually stopped.

Mike stepped out and approached the vehicle. As he got closer in the misty evening, he noticed to his astonishment that the van's back door was slid open, and the front passenger door was wide open. He ran to the front of the van, noting the driver's side door was also yawning open. The van was completely empty. He looked in and noticed the transmission was on "drive", and the van was moving very slowly on its own.

Quickly, Mike put the van in "park" and rushed back to Mark. He told him what he saw, and Mark exited the car to check around the bridge. They yelled a few times for anyone in the vicinity, thinking for some odd reason that the owners might have stopped to pause by the bridge.

The area was completely silent. Now spooked, they dove back to the safety of their car and pulled away, choosing to go to a local bar to reassess what had happened. They hoped that whoever had abandoned the vehicle would return later, and they could pull through and head home.

The men stopped at a local watering hole just a few minutes away, facing the river. As they parked in the busy parking lot filled with patrons, Mike mentioned that he appeared to have dropped his wallet, hopefully in the car. Mark stood and waited by the restaurant's door as he watched his friend return to the car yards away.

Mike opened the passenger side door and spotted his wallet on the floor of the car. He leaned down to pick it up, and as he pocketed it and straightened up, he was astonished to find it was morning. The parking lot was now empty, with only their car in its spot. Mike turned to find Mark with a look of disbelief on his face. He told him one minute he was standing in the light of the tavern; then he felt as though he fell asleep. When he winked again, it was daylight. They'd just lost an entire night of sleep.

A third case comes from four college students in their late teens out for a drive on a Friday evening. Two couples had just completed their final exams at the local community college and decided to drive around the town, as the other couple was from a different region of the town. It was well past midnight, as they'd had a late dinner. As they decided where to go, the driver of the car decided to head towards Peddlers' Village, a local tourist stop that hosted boutiques and unusual shops in a garden setting. En route there, driving on a well-traveled road, the girl in the back spotted red lights approaching the car.

The girl alerted the driver, who looked at his rearview mirror and indicated it was "odd". The lights were only a pinprick in the rearview, but seemed to be rapidly approaching until finally they girl started to become agitated. When the driver looked again at his mirror, he discovered that the red "orbs" were now only a few feet from his back bumper.

The "orbs" were bright red and had some type of "corona" around each one. One seemed larger than the others, which appeared from the back window as larger than a full moon. The others, which followed it, about three in number, were about the size of a quarter. They moved erratically like a swarm of bees after something sweet.

He turned the car right onto a small road. There was no traffic other than the bizarre lights. As he went down the small road, he turned on his high beams, as it had no streetlights. As the girl and the boy in the back seat turned to see if the orbs were following, they noted with relief that the orbs were gone. The driver observed the rearview and indicated he had shaken them off, but his passenger to his right exclaimed.

Ahead, on the narrow road, were the "orbs", stationary and hovering over the glistening pavement about two to three feet above it. The driver gunned the motor and passed the orbs merely inches away as the lights parted over his car.

Whatever the lights were, his beams seemed to have served as a signal, and these "orbs" followed them. Now panicked and yelling, the four students were frantic to shake off whatever the red orbs appeared to be. The driver turned onto a farm, past a barn, and hid behind one of the deserted buildings. He shut off the headlights this time and told everyone to be silent.

As they observed their surroundings, they noticed the orbs converging behind the barn they'd passed. Then, still holding their breaths, they surveyed for an exit. The girl in the back screeched that a "man" was approaching the car. The passenger near the driver pointed to a man in silhouette that seemed to be by the barn, observing them, his back to the orbs. As the man "floated" on approach, the girls started yelling for the driver to step on the gas and leave.

The driver turned on his headlights and drove over the grass and past the orbs – he said he must have been burning rubber as he drove over seventy back to the main road, where they never looked back until they had dropped off one of the girls who was a local.

23. CONCLUSION FOR THE ALAMEDA FAMILY

At this juncture, the narrative of the Alameda family ends with the previous chapter. It appears that the event that began with Neala and a black-veiled nun whose specter etched a skin-deep mark on her thigh appear to have preceded, if not foretold, a series of malignant and terrifying events. It ends with the hasty departure of Neala, taking a teen daughter with her to escape the clutches of martial law. For the family, it began a deep division in the wake of a disastrous government which did not see justice until two decades later with the overthrow of the Marcos regime. All around the neighborhood of San Juan and beyond, in the aftermath of WWII, the dead continue to haunt the living, continuing to bear witness to the brutal murder and atrocities of war. The first half of this book attests to how it affected ONE family, among thousands.

The Alamedas saw tragedy in the Little Baguio townhome and then again with bizarre and terrifying hauntings in the San Juan home in the aftermath of Ernest's suicide at the tender age of twenty-four. The bloody aftermath of war not only tainted the virgin soil on which the Alameda house was constructed, but the hamlet of Little Baguio which held a malevolent entity that later resembled the Mothman of Point Pleasant in the US. Less than five miles from each other, both homes remained dark and "heavy".

More significant was how it changed the personality of the patriarch of the Alameda household, Roberto Sr. His actions toward his unborn child appear to set the tone for further malice to take hold of the family in a very Roman Catholic nation. Culturally, all dead must be buried or it launches a curse by the victim whose rage sets fuel to a fire that may not die until all family members have atoned or been affected. It appears that this misfortune may even follow on foreign soil with the emigration of Neala as Neala sets to re-establish her career as a journalist in her new country with little if no success. Lisa grows up a teenager without the benefit of an extended family, finding a deeper spirituality in the interim and the long-term disenfranchisement a foreign country can bring.

FROM LISA'S lifetime journey punctuated by the unknown, I now enter a second part of the book focusing on other cases with less extensive detail and a focus on distinct events which were shared first-hand by the experiencer or witness themselves. During the period of time in which I traveled as an amateur travel photographer, I stumbled upon individuals who were either locals or vacationers who sought me after hearing of stories I shared with others. People are usually reluctant to share paranormal events for fear of ridicule, especially to strangers. However when people are thrust together as they are on a tour or in a foreign country as travelers, and they overhear ghost stories in a shared language over dinner, people tend to open up. It appears that in the context of a new environment, the strangeness of a new country, people are inclined to find solace by sharing unusual and sometimes terrifying experiences.

The stories flow even after dinner is done, over a fireplace, in the comfort of a hotel lounge, or outdoors in the safety of a crowded cafe. Numbers are exchanged and anonymity is guaranteed.

Thus, I now present to the reader the accounts from travelers far and wide and not so far, like the next town. I include those who travel often as well as first-time travelers. I also am happy to include those who trusted me enough: Those who find themselves living in the same area all their lives, or suddenly moving due to work or family pressure, some in remote regions and some in small towns. One lived in a large city. None of them have encountered anything beyond the normal thrumming of daily life, until then. It is these people who live such ordinary lives that when "something weird" happens, they are left to tell us in order to find meaning in the experience or to hear an explanation.

Please note that as you read the latter half of the book that the experiences as told to me are written here chronologically in the order in which I encountered these people. A few chapters return to the enigmatic figure of Lisa as she continues to keep in touch.

Enjoy the rest of the book in good health and abundance.

PART II

MY TRAVELS

24. THREE INTERNATIONAL CASES

From the years 1998 to 2015, I vacationed and toured several countries with my husband. Our travels were replete with cultural and culinary adventures. But during the leisure hours of the afternoon when the guides had left us on our own to do as we wished, my interest in the anomalous and bizarre, coupled with our natural gregariousness and benign openness, attracted locals and tourists who happened to encounter us.

When people seek to take in the atmosphere while resting at a café, curious locals will inevitably mingle, venture questions, and get to know the tourists. In this more carefree atmosphere where the opportunity to connect with locals presented itself, stories were exchanged. Fringe topics were not normally discussed at casual meetings, but somehow when people asked me my occupation as a writer, it inevitably leads to the question, "What do you write about?" Then stories flow, as they had with Lisa.

It was during a tour of Morocco in the early summer of 2004 where we found ourselves alone with the guides and driver that I heard of the "djinn" that a young woman encountered in the city of Marrakesh. Due to 9/11, American tourists were scarce in countries where Moslems were prevalent for fear of encountering with misadventure. Undeterred by such news, we toured Morocco for two weeks, finding ourselves the sole couple on the tour, to our delight.

We stayed at a major hotel in Marrakesh, replete with tile mosaics and authentic cuisine. The Berber guide, an excellent host, found his little group of two charming. He arranged to escort us through the city's souks, a busy hub of commerce where huge open-air and tented markets clustered adjacent to the city's square. "Monsieur Cloiseau", which we affectionately nicknamed the affable and informative gentleman, took us to the beautiful and grand historic sites, including, one afternoon, the oldest university in the Middle East.

Tucked in a quiet corner of Marrakesh and surrounded by narrow paved streets, the university's sole indicator of its presence is marked by a door set into the end of a very narrow alley with walls about fourteen feet high on both sides. The circuitous alleys, ancient and adobe in color, could be a maze even by day.

It was in this maze of streets, according to a vendor of dates, that a young woman encountered something that she could only describe as a "large dog" with "fangs". The creature was reportedly larger than the common stray dog occasionally found foraging the streets. "Larger", I was soon to discover, was about six feet in height when upright on its hind legs.

Around 9:30 p.m. in the evening, "Nimfa", as I will call her, had been studying in one of the university's classrooms, preparing for a test. She had emerged from one of the side doors of the university, which let her out into one of the darker alleys. During the evenings, lights were sparse in the area. As she approached a turn in the alley, she became inexplicably fraught with a sense of foreboding.

Clutching her books, she pulled her veil around her head

and made the turn towards the alley that led towards the main square. However, once she turned, she saw in the dim light from a nearby window something jet black, standing on two legs. Whatever it was had two red eyes and what appeared to be two ears on top of its head. It was at the end of the alley, yards from her but blocking her path. Nimfa was average in height by Moroccan standards for a woman, standing about five feet three. This creature at the end of the alley appeared taller than her by at least a foot. What was most alarming was that it was standing on its hind legs like a human.

About the size of a man, the girl thought. Alone, she swiftly turned in the other direction, seeking a means to avoid the creature. Then, behind her, she heard growling. She looked back from where she came, and that was when she saw it was following her. It was a large wolflike dog, teeth showing in menace. The creature was still standing on its hind legs, watching her.

She ran. She dared not look back, but she sensed it was in pursuit. At the university's door, she hoped the door wasn't locked. A young man exited as she arrived at the door, to her relief. As she hurriedly told him to go back in, he saw behind her a few feet away, an animal that dissolved into a whirl of black smoke, like a column of a small tornado.

A few students, believing she was sincere, as they knew her, came out to investigate. They were told later by an older man who sold goods nearby that the creature had been spotted before and usually appeared in the lonely alleys. He called it a "djinn".

During a tour of Budapest, Hungary, which was part of an Eastern Europe tour, we dined with a couple who sat with us in the dining hall of one of the hotels. They recounted their unusual encounter while vacationing in the south of France when they chose to rent a cottage that was part of a farm.

"Myra" and "Bill" were a middle-aged couple who retired early from their own business. Enjoying each other's company despite years of working together, they decided to depart from the chaos and busyness of tour groups by taking a leisurely independent vacation. They found a charming French cottage attached to a barn in the French countryside near the medieval town of Carcassonne. Besides an occasional housekeeper who came every few days, the couple was alone on the farm. Left with a list of local off-the-beaten-path places to dine, shop, and hopefully find a map to connect them to the next town, they were very much on their own.

Taking day trips in a rented Citroen and arriving in time to dine at local restaurants in the area, Bill and Myra decided one day to venture further south in hopes of strolling a beach. One afternoon, after an unexpected rain shower, they decided to leave the car at a local train station and proceed to a major tourist spot an hour away by train.

By the time they caught the local train back to the village near the farm and drove home, it was past midnight. As they parked their car late that night, they noted the lights were all out inside the cottage and at the front door, which they usually left on in the interest of security.

Bill, a very "tuned in" type of person, indicated that because of a previous incident in their home in the States, he had installed security there and was more sensitive to locking doors than ever before. Their home had been burglarized and the items never recovered by the police. One of the measures they'd taken was to install motion sensors around their property since they also lived in a remote section of their upscale town.

This farm was located about a mile from a small and charming village, very much on the rural side. However, unlike Bill's sensitivity to security, the owner of the current dwelling was not, as the area was very safe and far removed from crime.

After trolling the websites of rentals in the area, he found this one economical, though not as sought after, as it was remote to tourist spots on the French map.

Without the lights within and outside the house, Bill's head-lights penetrated the darkness, and he noted as the car swung to the front of the house that the barn next to it was wide open, which he distinctly recalled had been shut. Within the barn, there was a light of some type, bluish in color.

Myra suggested that the landlord must have dropped in, noticed that the lights were all on and, in their way of saving money, shut the lights off. She indicated that the landlord might still be in the barn for some reason at this late hour or left the light on in the barn by accident. They conjectured and traded theories, but nevertheless knew they had to check into the situa-tion. It was around 1 a.m. in the morning at that point, Bill noted.

Theories aside, Bill stepped out of the car, admonishing the curious Myra to stay in the car and lock the doors until his signal. He trudged toward the barn, approaching quietly from the side, watching its eerie light, reluctant to enter. He paused behind the open door and peered in through the slats. After a few minutes of scrutiny, he could not discern the odd light or its source. Still perplexed, his instinct towards self-preservation kicked in. Bill dashed back to the car as Myra disengaged the locks, and she stepped out. Bill signaled to Myra to run towards the house.

Myra quickly stepped out of the car and bolted for the rela-tive security of the house. They unlocked the door, entered, and locked it behind them anxious to inspect what might be amiss, if anything. After walking through the entire house, they conjec-tured that since nothing was missing or had been moved, the lights might have been tripped by a power outage or, as they thought, the landlord shut it off. Myra dialed the house phone, hoping to reach the landlord, but Bill pointed to the clock on the wall, indicating the lateness of the hour. They could be asleep. She hung up.

The couple retired to bed, dismissing the bluish light inside the barn, now worn out from their day trip and the stress of the late arrival. Bill joined his wife on the cool bed, covering themselves with the duvet. Myra had just shut the light off by her bedside when Bill, who felt he had just dozed off, felt Myra shaking him awake. She had been keyed up by the events of the day and decided to calm herself down by reading before going to bed, but she couldn't sleep. She had turned on the bedside lamp again, feeling uneasy, and as she reached for the book, she noticed the barn's light had intensified and was flickering as if on fire. She indicated that she noted the light they had seen before was somehow intensified, like it was just outside the bedroom window. Bill got up, approached the window, pushed the curtain aside, and looked out. From the bed, Myra reproached him, telling him to keep his head inside the window.

He turned to tell her it was just deer roaming outside. The barn was in complete darkness. Mystified, Myra got up, joined him at the window, and saw what she thought were deer as well. As she watched and observed, she noticed the "deer" were bipedal – as if standing on their hind legs. Bill observed one approach the kitchen window beneath them – on its hind legs. Now perplexed, he dressed and ran down to the kitchen.

The couple became more and more excited as they told their story in the hotel's lounge, where we finally moved to order drinks, absorbed in the narrative. Back to their story:

Through the kitchen window, the couple distinctly saw three creatures: The faces looked like deer staring in with a halo of blue behind them, similar to the light in the barn. They were on two legs, but no front legs appeared attached to their torsos. These "deer" were only about three yards from the couple's window. Shocked and terrified, Bill reached for the house's phone and dialed the owner, but got a message machine, and it was the manager's voice in French. Bill left a message anyway. The next day, they walked the area with the owner, who indicated that they'd never had a problem with prowlers. There were no prints on the grass, and the owner had not been there to turn on any light in the adjacent barn.

Nothing was amiss inside the barn, and the owner locked it. A day later, the couple relocated to the local inn in town, where a few of the locals who'd moved from the UK talked about strange "beings" roaming their fields.

A third story comes from a Thai couple who work and live as tenant farmers in a banana and rice plantation an hour outside Chang Mai, in the province of Lamphun. Our local guide during an escorted tour told this story when one afternoon, a couple of the tourists ventured away from the group. They ended up lost near a desolate road leading to a jungle and had taken a few hours to reorient themselves and find their way back to us. He shared a cautionary tale that tourists will never forget upon their return as we collectively sat down to dinner.

"Tia" and "Paul" live in a nipa hut on stilts at the center of the banana plantation they tended. The area was composed of eighty hectares of land, which they were responsible for maintaining, planting and harvesting along with two other farm families who live in similar dwellings. They also lived off the land except for occasional visits to purchase fish and other staples in the town's open market.

Tia and Paul had a baby – a boy. Doting on the infant, they placed him on a homespun crib in the one and only bedroom in the two-room shack. The hut was made of the traditional materials available in Southeast Asian farms: bamboo for a frame and strong "abaca", a fiber that can be made into rope and finished with banana leaves – the latter offered shelter and insulation from the sun and torrential rains. The hay and the banana leaves made for a roof crisscrossed by bamboo and lashed securely by the abaca ropes. These huts were elevated at least three feet from the ground to prevent floods from entering as well as any snakes and monitor lizards, which were abundant in that region.

Otherwise open to the elements, the huts were usually square in shape with a window on each side to allow for maximum ventilation from the tropical and highly humid heat. These windows were large and easily shut by a flap made of the same material as the walls and held open by a bamboo pole. There were no screens to protect from insects.

One evening, as Tia settled the child into the homemade crib by the open window, she covered the child's crib with a mosquito net, as the hut was open to the night's breeze, and flies and mosquitoes were abundant.

She went back to the main room of the two-room house and noted she needed to gather some water for the dinner preparation. Paul's return from the fields also usually meant he needed to wash before sitting to dinner. Reluctant to leave the infant alone, Tia nevertheless stepped out and gathered the empty pails and walked several yards to the pump that they used to irrigate the fields.

Since her husband was due back any minute, she anticipated that her infant, affectionately nicknamed "Beboy", would not be alone for a long period of time. They were in a remote part of the plantation, so no one would know their location except friends, some neighbors and, of course, the landowner and their parents, who all lived in the town.

As Tia stepped down from the hut, she carried the two pails on a long bamboo stick, balancing them to allow her maximum comfort. She noted it was getting dark. Halfway to the water pump, which was in an open area of the field several yards away, she noticed bats swooping under the coconut trees and palms.

Part of her wondered with concern whether she should have shut all the windows in the hut before she left.

Meanwhile, true to Tia's anticipation, Paul had returned, calling her name. Instead, he was greeted by gurgling from the infant in the next room, and he entered and smiled at the still form under the mosquito net, not bothering to uncover it.

Minutes went by as Paul tended to the sole gas stove in the kitchen, preparing it for Tia's cooking. He had just scooped rice for boiling when Tia entered the hut with two brimming pails of fresh water from the pump. As soon as she placed the pails down, they heard an unearthly screech like a banshee issue from Beboy's room.

Tia dashed to the room. She pulled the mosquito net away and discovered her biggest nightmare had occurred. Paul entered behind her as he heard her scream the scream of a distressed mother. In the crib was a creature the size of Beboy, but instead of his cherubim face, the face was of a wizened and angry creature only seen in horror movies, with teeth like that of a wolf. His mouth was full of razor-sharp teeth, his eyes red and glistening with anger. He looked aged and wizened.

Tia fainted, and Paul watched the creature get up on two wrinkled legs and leap out the open window. Paul believes to this day that the creature had abducted or eaten his infant son. It had perhaps lain in wait for them to leave Beboy alone.

Legends abound in Southeast Asia of a creature called a "Tiyanak": a demonic entity from within the earth that manifests as an infant to unsuspecting individuals. It is rumored to abduct babies to feast on their blood only to leave them dead or transformed into the creature this couple encountered in their son's crib. Despite an extensive search by the townspeople, they never found their infant son or his remains. Eventually, distraught with the memories of the tragedy, the couple left the plantation for another job, this time near Tia's parents.

25. THE DEMON AND A DYING MOTHER

About two hundred miles south of Manila, a small university town sits at the edge of a large mountain on the island of Luzon. This town, which will remain unnamed to protect it from curiosity-seekers who might deter future students from applying, has approximately 1,500 inhabitants. More a village than a town, it hosts the most abundant areas of local plant and wildlife. Surrounded by farms and tropical forest, the college is a rice research institute, a school of agriculture and a training ground for veterinary medicine. The college itself is old, established like the village it sits on; the campus, a site of massacres in World War II when the Japanese infiltrated the village and plundered homes.

Just steps from the fringes of the dormitories lies the sub-rural homes built for the professors and employees of the university. One of these neighborhoods sits at the crossroads of what was the site of a major massacre that butchered the villagers in the dead of night as they fled from their homes.

One of these houses is a continual witness to the ghosts and entities that haunt the village. As the story unfolds, the reader may come to the conclusion in light of the involvement of the

Holy Bible in this particular event that it may actually be a demon that came to visit upon this house.

Deeply religious as a Roman Catholic and devoted to the Holy Mother, "Sandy" was married for several years, and the marriage produced four children. As the story goes, she developed a heart condition early in her fifties upon her husband's sudden departure to live with a younger woman he had met while traveling overseas. As the chaos in the home ensued with his choice to leave the otherwise happy family, Sandy's health suffered and progressed to a heart condition.

As her illness progressed, Sandy became more devout, reportedly kind to a flaw and generous beyond anyone's belief. She donated her time to the church and was immensely devoted to her children and one granddaughter, whom she almost spoiled. Sandy was seen as a very benign, open and loving person among relatives, friends and the community she lived in.

The family, her children in particular, felt that Sandy's spiritual growth and consequent benevolence was a challenge to the demon, who find kind people whose righteousness to be steadfast and close to God a major challenge to convert. Some of the relatives felt that this type of person, where temptations fail, become an object of hatred and malign intent by the devil in his frustrated attempt to turn the good to evil.

Sandy's four grown children, none of whom were home at the time of the incident, had no idea what was to visit on the home one weekend night. Since Sandy had grown breathless with each passing day, her visits to the hospital more frequent for oxygen, she elected to stay home instead of joining her children when they went out to the town.

On this particular night, it was well past 9 p.m., which is still considered early for a tropical climate where the heat was still dissipating. Sandy decided to sit in the family room adjacent to the living room and watch a movie, her rosary and Bible on the coffee table. As she turned down the volume on the set, sensing something or someone peering into the living room window a few yards from the family room, she felt a cold chill issue from the window. As she turned to glance toward the living room and window beyond, she saw something as dark as night glaring back at her, sitting on the living room sofa – inside the house.

It was a being the size of a man, with horns and red eyes, so hateful and malevolent that Sandy instantly stood up in horror and disbelief. Moving away from the family room, Sandy grabbed her rosary as the being stood and approached her in pursuit.

On her way out of the room, Sandy grabbed the Bible on the coffee table and hurled it at the being and turned to run. It made the being furious. Undeterred, it flew towards the family room in pursuit, catching the Bible and tearing the book in half, scattering the pages. Sandy, now breathless from the sudden stress, made for her bedroom in the back of the house, where there was a cross on the wall. She ran past the dining room, then the kitchen as the being noiselessly pursued her.

She reached the bedroom, slammed the door and, clutching her rosary, prayed in earnest. Outside, her two sons had just arrived in time to see the being chasing their mother into the dining room. They entered through the courtyard door and confronted the being as it stood stopped at their mother's bedroom door.

Rick and Mike (aliases) yelled at the being to leave, which they reported as an amorphous black mass with red glaring eyes and the suggestion of horns on its head. It fled as Mike chased it, back to the living room and through the same window where Sandy had first sensed it.

When the boys checked their mother, they found Sandy clutching her rosary, sitting on the edge of her bed. They looked up at the cross above the headboard. They felt the being had left not because of them, but because Sandy had begun to pray. She told them she sensed a gentle presence in the room that was protecting her.

The being never returned. Months later, Sandy passed from heart failure.

26. THE VILLAGE MASSACRE AND SILVER HALL

After Sandy's passing, three of her children remained living in the house. During that time, the older of the two sons, whom I will call "Mike", unmarried with child, witnessed several uncanny incidents where he slept in the back corner of the house. The atmosphere drastically changes once night takes hold and the college students have long retired to their dorms or left for home. During Mike's stay in his parents' house, not only would he encounter ghosts, but he would hear stories of beings that roamed the university's buildings. One of these stories involved the university gymnasium just five minutes from the house.

An agrarian village before and after World War II, this university town was a center for botanists, photographers and a panoply of professors who loved the pastoral but upbeat atmosphere of a major university. The university, however, had a very tragic history for the role it played as an unwilling POW camp – particularly, the gymnasium and theatre inside it, which was one large building of three floors, which I will call "Silver Hall".

Silver Hall faced the quadrangle, enveloped in palm trees,

which swayed to the tropical breeze by day but lent a sinister air by night. Most students, well aware of its tragic history, walk in pairs when traversing its halls at night and are wary of staying back, particularly anywhere near the building.

Former students tell of the sounds of agony that can be heard late into the night issuing from its second-story windows. The building was the site of torture, interrogation and mass killings of not just soldiers, but clergy who stood against the Japanese.

The entrance of Silver Hall opens to a wide expanse of basketball courts, followed by a sizeable stage where theatre students practice. Due to the lack of space, student activities were straddled during the day and evening to accommodate both sporting events, practices and theatre rehearsals. In a rare opportunity, thespians shared a building with athletes. The stage existed as it was during the war, and its wooden floor tells a story. Forced to march in a circle on the stage, row upon row of priests were beheaded by the Japanese soldiers on this stage, their blood spilling onto the cement floor at the foot of the stage. The stains of blood reportedly still show sometimes at night, sometimes as early as dusk, bearing testimony to the tragedy.

The story goes that this "march" around the stage, which the priests were forced to form and circle and point to the next victim, reenacts itself to certain students. Alumni talk about the night when they saw, during a reunion of English majors, a group of priests walking in a circle on stage – without heads. One time, Mike examined the stage. He noted that in the back, where actors and actresses ascend the stage behind the curtain, is an open stairway leading to the basement. Lumber and old chairs had been strewn at its bottom, preventing passage.

On a visit to the area, I inquired of two alumni who willingly took me to the building and the reputedly haunted stairway behind the stage. They indicated that custodians had placed it there to deter new students from entering the basement area where most of the tortures took place. It was reportedly inhabited by "evil", and was a portal for mishaps to occur given its violent history.

As I roamed the area in the company of the two alumni, I took photos of the basketball courts as well. In one of them, the photo revealed orbs. I examined another photo taken by a different camera one of the alumni had taken with her and discovered more orbs following them as they walked.

I stayed for a month in Manila and visited Mike and his sisters, who continued to live there with his teenage daughter. The women eagerly told me of the paranormal events after he himself encountered something surreal one night at 1 a.m. as he was retiring to bed after an evening out with his girlfriend. However, Mike would not discuss what he encountered, and as I was planning to investigate the home, intrigued by the story of his mother Sandy's encounter, he decided he would hold back and allow me to "sense" the house so as to allow for an unbiased opinion.

Across the hall from the bedroom where Mike slept was another bedroom, now used as storage for surplus clothes. This room had a history as well. On the other side of this storage bedroom was a full bath, which connected to Sandy's former bedroom, now Sandy's second daughter's room. It was shared by Mike's daughter, Sandy's granddaughter at the time of my visit. Being a good host, Mike had offered to vacate his room so that I might stay there for the duration of the visit, as Manila was over two hundred miles north. Little did I know how haunted Mike's room was.

Around 1 a.m., I awakened to a series of yells and screams issuing from the street beyond. The patter of running feet, a sense of chaos, and a general feeling of upheaval accompanied the sounds. I pulled away the covers, wondering what was afoot.

Above me to the right was a large window with the house's cement wall a few feet away. Beyond the wall was a faint streetlight.

Outside, I heard the distinct sound of marching feet headed my way. Whoever they were, they were booted and marching like soldiers, the sound becoming more pronounced by the minute. It was headed for the street right outside the window. More screams, alarm, panic, chaos. I sat bolt straight, now alarmed by the sounds, which had increased in volume and alarm.

I looked around me in the dark, attempting to locate the lamp. I wondered why the other occupants of the house had not heard at this point, as the ruckus was very loud and chaotic. Suddenly, the marching stopped by the wall adjacent to my window. The wall itself has an upper part with wrought-iron rails cemented into the top of the wall for good measure. Someone threw what sounded like heavy chains on top of the wrought iron, and the chain caught the grillwork.

Then I heard what I surmised was a group of men pulling or tugging at the wrought iron, as if to take down the wall. The sound was so loud that I stood from the bed and finally made to peer out the window. I reached for the light, flicked it on, and all the sounds suddenly stopped. Surprised, I reached for the window, pulled one section of the glass open, and yelled, "Who goes there?!"

No reply. The street was quiet, as if abandoned suddenly. Total silence. I felt my skin crawl as I proceeded to leave the room and walk to the kitchen for a drink. The house was deathly silent.

The next morning, when I sat down to breakfast with Mike and his sisters, I related the events of the evening before. The siblings glanced at each other and told me that they too had heard that before and many others who had visited and slept overnight. Some had left the next morning, wondering if there was a fire or some emergency and, upon being told it was a haunting, left swiftly for a hotel or inn in town.

Mike now knew he wasn't dreaming. He'd had the same exact experience at the same time of night every year on the anniversary of the massacre. Last night had been the anniversary of the massacre when Japanese troops entered the village and plundered the homes, killing men and raping the women. Townspeople were fleeing for their lives in the dead of night, without prior warning. Dressed in nightclothes, they carried what they could of their belongings or locked themselves in, only to have walls and doors pulled down by chains. That was what I had heard: chains being dragged and used as a way to take down a wall crowned with iron rails.

My encounter was a re-enactment of the mad dash to safety, the entrance of the soldiers, and the phantom chains, which attempted to pull down the grillwork of the phantom cement wall near me. As I elected to stay the week despite the experience, I would later become acquainted with the other rooms of the house and its other specters.

Dr. and Mrs. Alameda on liberation day.

Adelaida, aged seventeen. Paco Laguna, Philippines.

Dr. Alameda in military uniform.

Ernesto (right), looking at Lisa's christening. His closest brother, Bing (left), served as godfather.

Alameda and siblings on vacation.

Roberto Junior, college graduation photo.

The haunted armoire. Note the shadow of a Japanese helmet resting on top of the windowsill. Photo courtesy of "Mike".

The road where the red orbs chased the students.

The pond where the red orbs reappeared. Author's photo.

Marrakesh: The alley where the djinn appeared to a young girl. The door to the oldest university is at the end. Author's photo.

The Marrakesh djinn disappeared in a whirl of smoke right by this archway.
Author's photo.

The 9/11 Memorial Park steel reinforcement. Note the
shadow by the feet in the upper area of the photo. Compare
the face to the one in the armoire mirror. Photo courtesy Dee
Maier.

The lake water reflection taken by Dee Maier. Note the "mist" above the unknown blue object under the water.

The "Silver Hall" haunted stage (backstairs) leading to the basement where torture took place during WWII. Author's photo.

The author in Carcassonne, a few miles from the sighting of the "standing deer" seen by a couple on holiday.

27. THE "KAPRE", THE MAN IN THE BED AND THE ARMOIRE MIRROR

P hilippine folklore runs deep in the subrural areas south and well north of Manila. One of these phantoms that have been witnessed time and again through the years is the "kapre", or tree demon.

My stay at the home of Mike and his sisters was replete with stories, coupled with my own sense of being watched, particularly at night. My sensitivity to things at the edge of my vision led to a feeling among my hosts that they were free to tell of their uncanny experiences in the house. Free from possible ridicule in the safety of an open listener who had now herself experienced a haunting in the home from just a few nights before, the hosts opened up. The story about their ailing mother was just a beginning.

Lunch during the weekends and even dinner was an open forum for catching up on relatives far and wide. Those stories inevitably led to their own bizarre encounters with the unknown. One evening, as the family sat down to dinner, usually later in the evening, they were alarmed by the scattering of the domestic cats in the courtyard.

The breakfast room, which was less formal and more relaxed

than the adjacent dining room, was usually the center of the household. Close to the kitchen, which had an internal adjoining window where food was passed through, the breakfast room was sunny but hot during the day, as it had one wall completely glassed and afforded a view of the entire courtyard beyond. However, at night the coolness of the room with a fan on one side made for a comfortable spot for dining.

The house had a courtyard on one side, which was accessible from the gate and the carport. Potted plants decorated the walls, and large trees dotted the inside walls. One end closest to the open laundry area in the rear of the house was an annex, which contained their father's former darkroom on the second floor, and the first floor doubled as the washer and dryer area for any laundry that could not be hung in the outer laundry.

In the courtyard, the maid fed the feral cats in the open late at night and watered the numerous tropical plants. On one edge of the courtyard, a tree that had been there previous to the house's construction had been walled in to encompass part of the garden. It was this tree where a manifestation was repeatedly sighted at night.

One evening, as the group gathered to share the dinner meal, I sensed something staring at me as I sat at the table facing the large glass window. Only separated by the glass and the wooden blinds, which were left open, I surveyed the dark area where only the outside lights could penetrate.

Past the courtyard, two pinpricks of what seemed like eyes glared back at me from within the branches of the large tree. Mike had just sat down across from me with his back to the window, when he observed me pause eating. He turned and looked at the tree behind him. The group retold of a strange being who inhabited the tree and could be seen when there was a visitor in the house. It was considered a kapre, as it seemed to be protecting the tree and the surrounding garden from strangers.

Reportedly, the kapre is a spirit, an elemental, who scares predators away as a protective gesture. It appears as a bipedal creature with only a suggestion of its appearance: A narrow head, large menacing eyes, a body that appears to meld into the trunk of the tree, and knees protruding to suggest that it is hunched, ready to spring. Sometimes, as it was that evening, only the face can be seen, particularly the eyes.

To "scare" it away, the group laughed loudly and turned up the television in the family room, markedly changing the atmosphere from gloom to merriment. In a few seconds, it disappeared. As with negative beings, laughter, gaiety and merriment chased them away, the emotion incompatible with fear and melancholy.

Two other hauntings manifest inside the house. These discarnate beings predate the home and may have been ghosts from the massacre. At the rear of the house, the first bedroom on the right where I stayed, is where the marching Japanese soldiers were heard in the previous chapter. The next bedroom, mentioned before as being in the center of the rear, is where two of the women shared one of the larger bedrooms. This bedroom has been changed to a storeroom of sorts after repeat episodes of something very frightening.

One of the sisters, "Alicia", usually retired to bed earlier than the other since she went to work rather early. For this reason, she always fell asleep before her sister retired to the bed near her usually after the late movies were over. On this particular night, she went to sleep alone once again, as her sister had gone to a party and would was not expected to return until much later. Due to closet space restrictions in the bedroom, they'd purchased an armoire and placed it on the other side of the room on the same wall as the main bath. This made space a premium, so it was decided that the beds be pushed together to economize on space.

As the story goes, Alicia dozed off into a deep sleep, only to be awakened by someone intently looking at her. She had had this feeling before as she did with the kapre in the courtyard, but never saw anything. This time, with the other bed pushed against her own, she opened her eyes against her own counsel and beheld a man, gaunt and frightening, leering at her from the next bed. "He" was just inches from her face, lying prone on her sister's bed on his side. He looked emaciated and was wearing what seemed a bloodied tee shirt.

Alicia shot up from the bed in terror. The man continued to leer at her with such menace that it drove through her being like a bolt of cold lightning. She turned and could not pull the door open fast enough to exit to the corridor. There, she ran to the family room, to the consternation of her brother, who sat watching TV – the volume turned low so as not to disturb her. She told him what had happened, and the next night she moved into Sandy's room, her mother's former bedroom, and camped by her niece's bed. It was the only room in the house, prayed over and blessed, that was not haunted. It was around that time that Mike's bedroom had the sounds of the massacre and the marching soldiers, which he had first overheard in the dead of night.

The youngest of the four children, whom we will call "Rick", was married and was renting a flat. Since they were expecting a child, the siblings offered for them to stay temporarily in the house, as Alicia months later moved out and joined her boyfriend to rent a flat downtown. This was after my weeklong visit. The oldest, "Dana", had left the room as well and moved into the fourth bedroom behind the family room, afraid of being alone in the room. In the fourth bedroom, she joined the live-in maid for company.

No one told the unsuspecting wife, "Liz", who at the time was a few months pregnant with Rick's child. The couple were happy to accept the offer, as they were saving for the baby and put the rent money aside when they moved in. So move in they did, right into the sisters' abandoned bedroom, noting that they were sandwiched between Rick on one side across the hall and the main bath on the other, which adjoined the niece's room. It seemed a great temporary arrangement until a more permanent home could be found.

From the first night forward until they left two years later, Liz would deal with both the sounds of the massacre, which she heard from the bedroom window, and, one night, one chilling specter she would not forget – and it was not the leering man.

Heavy with pregnancy, Liz retired early to read a book, hoping to unwind and fall asleep. She was working full time at a bank, and the stress of standing on her feet all day had made her back ache. With dinner put away and her part of the chores done, she slipped away from the family and donned her night-gown, entering the room alone.

As Liz prepared for a relaxed sleep, she shut the lamps off in the room and left the door ajar for her husband to enter. She reported a breeze, colder than usual, enter the room from the hall. She recalled the haunted bedroom across the hall, where the sounds of marching were more pronounced, and got up quickly to shut the door. As she clambered back to bed, she saw at the foot of the bed against the wall an image of a woman clad in a nightshift. The image floated towards her, and she saw the woman had no legs. She screamed. Rick ran into the room, the second time he'd had to come to the rescue of a family member in the house after the event with his deceased mother. He saw nothing this time, as the specter had already dissipated, though Liz was shaking with fear. They started making plans to locate another dwelling shortly after that. An argument ensued with the rest of the family when Rick and Liz found out about Alicia's encounter. They called this specter "the Woman in White".

A third encounter involved a small room that served as a small bedroom for Mike's grandmother. In her twilight years, their grandmother was shuttled between her children's homes, and when she stayed with her daughter Sandy's family, she had stayed in this small fifth bedroom. Miniscule in size, it divided the family room from the main dining room; its door opened toward the office where Sandy's husband worked when he worked from home.

During the time of my visit, this bedroom was long abandoned by the grandmother, who was reluctant to return to the room because of an issue with the armoire that she'd brought with her from her own home. She felt the armoire and its mirror inside were haunted. Her daughter and youngest son would check the armoire repeatedly, as she insisted that the mirror inside was "possessed". Eventually, the grandmother passed away from old age in the neighboring town of Pagsanjan, in the home where her husband had been born and raised.

Years later, Sandy and her grown children used the room as a closet, stowing away used clothing and all sorts of kitchen stuff they hardly used. They periodically used the armoire for the linen and dining napkins used for festivities. One day, her oldest daughter opened the armoire door to check her new outfit, as the inside had a full-length mirror attached to the door.

To her consternation, Dana looked not at her reflection, but that of a wizened old woman, frail and terrifying. The woman appeared starved to death. Immediately, she slammed the armoire's door, heedless of its antique value. In terror, she bolted from the small room and announced that she had found a "portal" in the small room. By week's end, the smallest room in the house had been christened a portal.

Out of curiosity, each family member would march in during

the day to check and recheck the mirror inside the armoire, but it was at nighttime when it was most sinister, when an unsuspecting guest would enter the room to use the mirror within and find the reflection of someone other than themselves. The same room had a small window, which opened to the family room, and legend has it that sometimes they see someone peering out when a good film is showing late at night.

28. ROBERTO'S ANCESTRAL HOME

In the rural province of Pagsanjan (pronounced "Pug-san-hon"), sits a two-story Spanish colonial home on the main road. Just a few yards from the epicenter of activity, it was built around 1838. The home was constructed in the fashion of typical Filipino homes during those days: Heavy wide wooden floorboards were secured with wooden pegs, and fourteen-foot-high walls connect to ornate designs on the ceiling. The last few feet where the wall met the ceiling was ornately cut out with fili-gree, allowing the warm air that rose to pass through the rooms and out the open windows.

Back then, kitchens were constructed to last, the counter completely made from tile and cement, with the large sink made from the same materials. All perishable goods were stored in the lowest part of the house, the ground floor, where a pantry opened to a cut in the ground where stone covered the cold floor. This house was no exception: The cool morning and evening breezes wafted freely through the second floor, and the ground floor stored grain, rice, and foodstuffs, and a large "refrigerator" was a hewn area below the cement and secured with a stone slab.

Parties happened often in those days: Fiestas commemorating saints and the Virgin Mary, whose feast day was
commemorated with a lavish town parade, and the births,
anniversaries, and weddings were huge affairs that merited an
entire week of preparations and another week of celebrations.
This was the atmosphere of post-war Manila and the small
towns that surrounded it after the building boom, which
heralded prosperity and a love of gaiety and merriment.

In the Pagsanjan home, the newly built home was grand for
its day. It was a source of pride for the one and only family who
ever lived there until 1958. Lisa's great-grandfather was a
landowner who ran an abaca plantation and a rice field with
over sixty hectares of land. He had two growing sons. Roberto,
the older of the two, seemed destined for a science career with a
keen interest in medicine. The younger would run the plantation upon his father's death. Juana, their mother, was a young,
diminutive woman with captivating eyes and a sweet and shy
disposition.

The house had two floors; the kitchen in the back opened to
a verandah, which doubled as an open pantry. Upstairs, the
veranda had a stone balcony, which afforded a view of the huge
backyard resplendent with fruit trees. The kitchen, where
servants slept in an alcove, connected to a formal dining area
and an adjoining drawing and living room, which faced the
front of the house. In its time, the street was relatively quiet,
punctuated by horse hooves as "*calesas*", or horse-drawn
carriages, passed by.

The townspeople were educated and reserved, polite and
gracious to strangers. They kept the town clean and were close-
knit, but not hostile to outsiders nor foreigners. As a matter of
fact, they were frequented by tourists overseas. The town was a
sought-after tourist destination for its nearby waterfall and
wildlife, intricate embroidery and local sweets.

Before and after World War II, far and away from the Japanese destruction wrought on Los Banos, the town was frequently visited by European tourists who hailed from the far reaches of Scandinavia, Switzerland and Germany. The unique backdrop of a Southeast Asian country infused with Spanish colonial culture and the flora and fauna of a rainforest made the area unique and one of a kind.

Juana lavished attention on the home. An avid plant lover, she spent her days tending the extensive fruit garden in the back; a profusion of orchids in pots lined the external stone stairwell leading up to the second floor, where a second living room was located for houseguests. She was on her own for much of the week, as her husband watched over the tenant farmers who tilled and harvested the extensive fields of abaca and rice.

Despite the size of the rectangular home, it appeared small from the road, as it was built with the longer end spanning the lot to the back. An extensive network of large windows spanned both sides, with a verandah on both floors opening to the back.

In the cool late evenings, Juana and Celso sat in the verandah – one reading books and the other the daily newspapers. The radio was a large device, which gave them news from all over, particularly the station Radio Veritas, one of the first of its kind to share international news. It was this station that told the couple the advent of the First World War. They listened from afar as the world unraveled, relatively unaffected in their haven of safety in the remote but first-class town. But this idyllic state was not to last, as Juana, in her mid-forties, was struck down by cancer. While Roberto and younger son Celso trained for their respective careers in medicine and business, Juana fought against a cancer when the treatment was still in its infancy.

Ravaged by the disease, she succumbed before she turned

fifty and was followed shortly by Lisa's great-grandfather, who grieved and died of a broken heart. Roberto and Celso agreed to part, the older son leaving his younger brother alone in the large house to worship the ghosts of their parents. Now without grandparents, Roberto took his wife and children one final time to visit his younger brother, and they agreed to visit as often as before. Sonya, the oldest, would miss her grandmother, who doted on her, though Neala did not, feeling chastised by the older woman for "faults" she could not control as a young child.

Like his father before him, Celso ran the farm with the assistance of a manager, rode a horse to oversee the fields, and tended the accounting. He sent his brother, now in the city of Manila with a practice, the fruits of their bounty: first-rate rice in bags made with the strong fiber of abaca. It would be a profitable exchange between brothers where Roberto rendered free healthcare for his brother and the tenant farmers in exchange for rice and an extensive harvest of fruit. Celso helped his brother's large family to know and appreciate fresh tropical fruit, ripened on the tree, as well as newly harvested rice, rich with minerals from the rich soil of Pagsanjan.

Years would pass in the now silent home as Celso remained a bachelor and landowner. One late night, settling in for the night, he forgot to shut off the lamp in the kitchen and ventured out toward the back of the house. In his light pajamas, Celso was small in size, after his mother, who had doted on him.

As Celso emerged from the bedroom and down the steps, he noted a figure in silhouette standing by a window in the kitchen. The smell of fresh coffee wafted past his nose. Living alone, he wondered if one of the tenant farmers had come to drop off some harvest at his door and had decided to stay for the night at this late hour.

As Celso approached the figure, he noted the silence despite the open windows, which gave respite from the oppressive heat and humidity. He felt his arms prickle with fear when he was about a few feet from the woman, who did not respond to his greeting of "*Kamusta po?*" (How are you?) Instead, he noted the woman's profile in the dim light as becoming increasingly familiar. A gasp involuntarily issued from his throat as he realized the specter was none other than his own mother. As soon as he recognized her, her specter faded.

Celso approached the window, looking out, wondering what had summoned his mother. With trepidation, he dashed out of the house, summoning the maid, who was in the outside pantry at the side of the house. The maid, nonplussed, had seen the specter before and told him that the woman was not malevolent – just watching after her own son who chose to remain a bachelor in the lonely old house.

29. THE ENCOUNTER ON ROUTE 263

B ack in the States, I had returned to document in a more formal fashion all the stories so far that had been shared with me. I had also attempted to secure photographs from witnesses, both UFO related or entity related. It proved to be a frustrating endeavor, as most are reluctant to share not only their identities and locations, but even photographs. In some photographs, such as those of the orbs I personally saw developed later on, I was told not to share them. To honor the witnesses' desire, I will refrain from sharing any that may identify the witness in the photograph.

These next encounters I personally experienced after I had returned from my visit to the Philippines.

In late fall of 2009, I was driving to work one early morning and had to take a detour due to some road construction, which had begun the day before. The roads were still dark and desolate, as it was only 5:50 a.m., way before traffic commenced on this well-traveled road. As I turned onto Route 263, which was a four-lane blacktop, I took the right lane and proceeded at forty-five mph. Several yards ahead of me, I noticed an unmistakably bright light high in the dark sky.

Unlike a commercial jet, this light was stationary. It appeared to hover in place as I approached, its size getting bigger by the second. Perplexed, I slowed down, trying to get my bearings, as I was approaching south, away from the town where I lived in Buckingham. Its shape was unlike the International Space Station, which presented or appeared cone-like in the dark sky. Furthermore, it was way too low to be the space station, from what I surmised. As I had no frame of reference in terms of size, I accelerated to where it would be just above me.

As I approached, I determined the light to be triangular, with a black band midway down the triangle. Now with a closer view, I observed the light from the object was not from the object itself, but appeared to be reflecting another source of light somewhere behind me. Alone on the road as best as I could determine, there was no one to corroborate my sighting. The object was completely still, silent and alien. I sensed it was intelligent, almost watching what I would do next. I could not sense its intent, nor could I get a "feel" of whether it was benevolent or malevolent. It was just there.

My car passed under it, and through the sunroof, I saw that it had a square base, matte black in the dim light. It was less than five hundred feet above my car. I felt a sense of foreboding as I passed, as if whatever it was knew I was examining it and was waiting.

I stepped on the gas and observed it in my rearview mirror as it came into view. It seemed to stay there, waiting for something. Perhaps it was observing me and the area as much as I was observing it.

Adjacent to the route was a large farm for crops, then a hill. On the other side of the route was a small community of homes still in slumber at that early hour. I turned at the next intersection, where I finally lost the object from view. I drove into town and stopped for coffee and told the bagel man who emerged from his back counter in the company of one of his employees. He pointed up at the sky and indicated that there had been something like a "large light" over one of the buildings.

I returned to the road upon my way home that afternoon and waited to hear any information from the local news. As I expected, there was nothing.

30. THE "SHIMMERING COMB", THE "TRIANGLES" AND ANOTHER VISIT

With a record increase of 700% of unknown objects reported in the sky in 2008, it was a matter of time before I joined a growing number of previous skeptics who would come to report a record number of encounters on the online database. In the small hamlet where I lived, sightings became a regular occurrence that summer and fall – and as the reader has seen in the previous chapter, I saw one with my own eyes even a year or so after the UFO flap was over.

Weeks passed. As frost took hold of the small town and the residential homes and farms at the edge of town still slept, I once again would have another encounter. I drove out of my residence situated inside a small cluster of homes perched on a hill overlooking the large farm I had previously mentioned. I turned down a two-lane road leading to a main road below, this time taking my customary route, driving on a narrower road, Route 202. As before, it was barely six in the morning; thus it was still night.

Ahead of me, the road curved downwards toward the center of the small hamlet where a convenience store, a Wawa, was situated. As I rolled down the hill and approached the intersection, I stepped on the brakes to stop at the light.

Immediately, I saw a large object hovering right above the Wawa convenience store. It was shimmering and changing colors from pastel blue to pink to green and, finally, to yellow and back. Whatever it was seemed shaped like a bent comb, rolling as it changed colors. Eyes riveted to the object, very alone in the dark intersection, I reached for my cell phone, which I had just charged.

The cell phone was dead. The light changed. I turned right onto Route 202, trying to digest what I'd just seen. Once again the street remained deserted, but ahead I saw a light through the trees on my left. This one was further away and was a plain white light, perhaps a jet. I accelerated, watching the time, as I was concerned I would be late for work.

As the road bent towards the right, I sensed I was being followed. My SUV skimmed the dark road as I ignored the prickling of the hairs on my neck. The road bent left, and I eased the SUV around, following the curve of the road. Right in front of me dead ahead, I saw a large light, the same one that I'd seen earlier through the trees. It was moving very fast, crossing the street, disappearing to my right.

I drove and ignored the light, keeping my eyes on the dark road only lit by my headlights. Once in a while a car would pass on the opposite side. I looked up and saw the object remained ahead to my right as if escorting me. I arrived once again at the bagelry and darted into the shop.

The owner, another UFO enthusiast, once again emerged, intrigued by the sightings from the year before. He emerged with another patron and an employee, and they all observed the light, which seemed to me to be the same one that had followed me along Route 202. Together they excluded the possibility it was the space station, but could not determine the nature of the light, which now appeared cone-shaped from their position on the sidewalk. It had to be the space station. The next day, the TV news crew arrived at the same time and interviewed the employee. The object was no longer in the sky the next morning at that same time.

Roughly a week later, I was driving early on a Saturday to purchase produce at an open market, since it was one of the last and final weekends when local farmers would sell for the season. Winter was coming, and with it, the street vendors stopped selling fresh produce and goods outdoors. Again down Route 263, I noted the same feeling and the same object as weeks before.

A large vertical triangle, bright silver, was hovering a few yards ahead of the car. It was definitely the triangle I had seen weeks before. A definite black "band" was across the triangle, so it appeared that the base was separate from the triangle's apex. Yet it appeared that it was one object as it hovered above me.

As I examined the object, I noted that it was stationary again, and my SUV seemed to be approaching it. This time as I passed under it, it paced the car, moving so that it remained fixed for a few minutes just within view. For what seemed like a few minutes, it shimmered and brightened as if to acknowledge me.

Then, when I was about twenty yards past it, the object shot up and disappeared from the sky. I continued driving, wishing my compass were on the seat. I didn't want to lose sight of it, but it just "zipped" up and disappeared. There were a few cars on the road with me, but no one seemed to notice the strange object.

A week after Hurricane Katrina, a storm that devastated the southeast areas of the United States, particularly the state of Louisiana, I was again on my way to work at 5:45 in the morning. The traffic was light in the aftermath of the storms, with ominous clouds converging – another portent of heavy rain.

As my SUV approached the intersection of Route 202 and Upper State Road right past the town of Doylestown, I looked ahead past the microwave tower and noted a formation of dark iron-gray clouds right above the tower. Approaching a four-way stop, I stepped lightly on the brakes, slowing to a halt less than five hundred yards from the intersection, with two cars ahead of me at a standstill.

Suddenly, from the heavy cloud right above the tower, a light, triangular in shape, broke through the cloud. It was immediately followed by two other lights of the same shape on either side of it. Between the three triangles, I discerned a metallic shape connecting the three lights, which appeared as an inverted bowl.

This time, better prepared for a sighting, as the object broke through the clouds, barely skimming the top of the tower, I reached for my compass in the glove compartment. With a dawning awareness that the object was unnatural for a helicopter or a small fixed-wing craft, I noted the compass now on the seat. It was spinning as the object flew within view of my sunroof above me, accompanied by an almost imperceptible sound resembling a rush of water.

As the traffic moved forward, I took one last look behind me, the object proceeding at five to ten mph toward the local hospital. Behind me, another woman in her car gaped and watched as well. When I finally proceeded to the stop sign, the cloud cover was as before with no suggestion of anything out of the ordinary. I reported the event to the online MUFON website.

31. THE "VOICE" AT THE CONDO

I n 2014, a year after Bobby's death from end-stage cardiac failure, Lisa visited her mother, Neala, who lives in Connecticut in a small village nestled in the woods. Neala, now in her late seventies, was living sequestered amidst books and periodicals. Neala's love of books and anything literature was evident in her extensive library.

As Lisa visited and joined her mother for dinner at the woman's small condo, fatigue overtook her after a three-hour train ride. After a simple meal, they watched a movie; then Lisa sought the refuge of the second bedroom, which served as a guest room.

As Lisa passed the hallway, headed towards the bedroom ahead, she heard a distinct male voice command, "Get out!" She instinctively turned to her right, where there was a temperature gauge on the wall. She stood, puzzled; then a sense of menace overtook her. She kept walking, surmising it must have been the TV in the living room.

As Lisa made the bed, she felt the temperature in the room plummet. Steam issued from her nostrils as if she were outside. She exited the room and checked the temperature on the same part of the wall as before – 70 degrees. Puzzled, she reentered the bedroom once again and felt the sudden change.

Pulling out a comforter, Lisa hurriedly climbed into the bed and then decided to pull the second comforter from the closet. Layering it on top of the first, she lay down, exhausted. She shut the light off near her.

Not two minutes had passed when she felt something sharp jab her in the back. Her eyes fluttered open with surprise. She sat up, turned and felt the mattress. The room was stone cold and felt oppressive. The mattress was smooth. Lisa lay down again, covering herself, attempting to keep warm.

Once again, a jab, then another. This time there were two sharp objects on her back. She shot up and realized there was something in the room, which had followed her from the hall. She immediately turned the light on and, examining the mattress, sensed a growing menace from somewhere in the room.

Once again, Lisa turned on the light. This time she pulled out her rosary, and kneeling with her face toward the mattress, she said the entire rosary out loud. As soon as she began with the third Hail Mary, the room perceptibly began to warm. Halfway through the rosary, she felt the malignancy disappear, to be replaced by peace and a sense of lightness.

Lisa ended the first mystery of the rosary, kissed the cross, and made the sign. She hung the entire set of beads over the bedpost, shut the lights off, and took the second comforter off the bed. Eventually, she realized she didn't even need the first comforter and removed it as well. When she awakened again, the sun's rays were filtering through the window.

Lisa did not have the heart to tell her mother the night's events, concerned the woman would worry and become frightened to be alone in the home. A month later, she told a family friend, who then must have told Neala. Lisa told the friend she was filled with dread at the thought of visiting again, staying in the room and sleeping on the mattress – for fear the malignancy would return with a vengeance. When she did return, she would discover the mattress had been removed and the bed disassembled. In its place was a brand-new daybed. She was armed with a blessed photo of Saint Anastasius, which she had received as a gift from a concerned friend.

To this day, Lisa does not know if the infestation had left with the old mattress, if her prayer worked to permanently remove it, or if the photo of Saint Anastasius scared the malignancy away. She sensed the condo was peaceful save for the disorder of books and periodicals, which were scattered all throughout the condo.

32. AN "EXAMINATION"

In the winter of 2017, as this book was being written, Lisa had another encounter that was not only puzzling, but singular in comparison to her previous experiences. After over twenty years working in a school, Lisa started making plans for an early retirement. While she enjoyed the company of the children and helping them surmount the multiple barriers they faced in the current times, she grew weary of the minutiae and politics, which made the job tedious.

Lisa grew restless, seeking a new avenue in her quest to fill the time with new knowledge and new pursuits. Since her stint as a UFO investigator, she had longed for something new to fill her time. One of the people she met was a chiropractor who engaged in alternative medicine – one of which was bioenergetics. Lisa's growing respect for the woman was staunched only by her lack of insurance, which only endorsed standard medicine. She found herself visiting her often in the first few years because of a bad back, but then as insurance would have it, she regrettably had to taper off the visits. In frustration, Lisa began to question the limits of conventional medicine and the ulterior motives of big pharma.

Lisa's growing discontent with the limits of conventional medicine and her growing reliance on alternative healing, and the effectiveness of prayer in the resolution of her bout with cancer, made her reluctant to seek medical help when she ended up with colds and even the flu. She faithfully returned to the chiropractor, whose thriving business and selfless acceptance of Lisa encouraged her even further to let go of insurance, which she felt was only there to feed the greed of large companies, always reluctant to pay out despite the large premiums.

Lisa embarked on organic toxic cleanses and emerged with much energy and vigor, dropping down to a mere twelve to fourteen pounds overweight. With her physical stamina much improved, she began to add jogging and running to her lifestyle. She added two more dogs to the household, and they rewarded her with the energy she needed in order to make the morning runs less lonely.

As her husband's health was diametrically opposite to Lisa's, she became more and more concerned with his health and longevity. Overweight by clinical definition, Lisa attempted to add fish and introduce more organic vegetables and fruits to a diet that was traditionally American. Lisa's love for foreign cuisine added a medley of authentic flavors to the dinner table, but when Lisa wanted to remove red meat, the husband rebelled.

One evening, at the height of Lisa's concerns over the health and well-being of her spouse, she fell asleep after her evening prayers, which included their continued wellness and prosperity. Her nightly ritual before the movies they watched proved extremely fruitful in ameliorating her issues at work regarding marginalization and discrimination.

This time, the continued prayer addressed the growing concern over their health in a unique way that did not surprise Lisa, but the unusual approach left her stunned.

As the evening progressed, Lisa retired to bed at the usual time that Thursday night, relaxed and happy that the weekend was close by. Her book on her nightstand waited for her and, she snuggled with it for an hour before she finally fell asleep.

About 2 a.m., Lisa sensed a presence in the bedroom and noted that her husband was snoring fitfully next to her. She recalled turning him to his side, which he obediently did, and the sounds of the night lulled him to sleep. As she lay faceup, she immediately fell fast asleep. However, not long after, she awakened when she felt a glass rod touch and make a sound as it "clinked" against her front teeth. Immediately, Lisa's eyes flew open. Myopic, she attempted to see above her, but failed to see anything.

She shifted and lay on her side, and that was when she saw just less than two feet from her bedside, a group of thin semi-translucent beings, with benevolent eyes. They were standing as a group. She sensed the group of beings waiting in silence for her reaction. She did not sense a malignancy nor any intent to do harm, but rather, an almost paternal presence. She got a sense that the beings in the room had been "examining" her and her spouse, but she awakened. She self-consciously touched her front teeth where the glass rod had touched, trying to discern if anything was amiss.

Lisa sensed a desire from whatever the presences were to intend her well-being. A desire for her and her husband to continue in health. Thus, it was almost like a medical checkup, which she had refused to do in waking life. Now, "they", whoever they were, had assumed the role for her.

As the next day wound down into evening, Lisa still pondered the motivation and nature of the visit. She knew it was not a dream, nor her imagination. This time, unlike the visit of the benevolent being during her year of cancer recovery, there was no visible mark left with a crucifix wound around her flannel nightgown button. The sound of the glass against her front teeth was unmistakable. She felt it and heard it as it made contact, manipulated by a very gentle hand, almost attempting tenderly not to intrude. For that, she was grateful and sensed a benevolence she could not reach for questioning or conversation. She longed for a return visit from the beings, hoping for some type of communication.

33. THE MOUND

As life would have it, people marry, get divorced, have children or remain childless, age, and eventually pass to the netherworld. Somewhere in the middle, those who remain divorced have their children to assist them in old age; some, though distant in emotion or geography, still call, send emails, text or whatever way they deem "contact". For others, children are a way of insuring that the next generation will remain on the planet.

For others who divorce or are widowed without children, the suddenness of being alone, anonymous, save for a few close friends and perhaps a myriad of acquaintances, the possibility of living alone or aging alone is a distinct possibility.

The next few stories come from that corner of reality where people find themselves, through their own doing or by the doing of another, navigating the world alone. Some take the solitude with a serene acceptance, managing their day-to-day affairs with a placid understanding of their own mortality and maintaining a meaningful busyness to keep their intellect alive through involvement in work and outside pursuits.

Some, like the next story that follows, launch on a furtive, if not desperate attempt to fill a void where silence and solitude appear to be dreaded, if not avoided at all costs. The following story is about the former type of individual, and it proved to conclude with some disastrous, if not evil results.

This riveting account of a life forcibly lived alone in a haunted location comes from a young man who chooses to remain anonymous. For the purposes of the story, we will call him "Paul." Paul walked into a neighborhood coffeehouse one day and sought to unburden his concerns to a few locals who were regulars at the establishment. His efforts to help his older sister rid herself of the evil that she appeared to have invited unwittingly had become futile, and he related the following story:

"Mae" lives alone in a small neighborhood by a river. Her home, part of the settlement of a divorce several years back, sits perched with its backyard facing a river that separates two states in the northeast corner of the United States. The stone house is over fifty years old, but well maintained. It sits on a modest half acre with a separate two-car garage. A high cement wall separates the home on both sides from its neighbors and from the edge of the river.

A view of the swiftly moving river can be seen from the second-floor bedrooms and through a wrought-iron gate that separates the garden backyard from the path leading to the river. The garden behind the house sits resplendent with giant cone-flowers hugging the path that leads to the water. Wisteria vines wind around the patio's whitewashed pergola, while wrought-iron chairs, also in white, lend a stable permanence to the field-stone floor of the patio.

Flash back to a decade ago, on a normal summer day, the river was replete with small yachts, fishing boats and motor-boats, as it was the height of the summer season. Sounds from the banks on either side of the river could sometimes be heard, as both sides of the bridge that connected them boasted a quantity of high-end Michelin and Zagat-merited restaurants. The area was a bustling tourist town where people from out of state and even out of the country frequented the area's quaint shops, boutiques, and bed-and-breakfast establishments. Picturesque and unique, Mae's home and the homes around her increased in value as the popularity of the area became known as a haven for artists, writers and fledgling filmmakers.

Inside the French doors past the fieldstone patio, above the cacophony of summer sounds, a man yelled and reprimanded a middle-aged woman with strawberry blonde hair. She was slim and of medium height, hunched over in defeat in a worn-out sweater. The woman was visibly upset, obviously on the verge of tears. She sat on a stool perched at the edge of a well-appointed, though small kitchen as the man in a leather vest, sporting a tattoo of a serpent, much taller than her, hovered and dominated the room with his gruff voice.

He bolted out of the kitchen, leaving Mae alone with her thoughts, still tremulous after the confrontation. The door slammed, and he rushed to the garage, pulled out his large motorcycle, and stepped on the kick-starter. Mae watched him as he roared out of the side driveway and past the open gate into the narrow street.

So was a typical day in Mae's life. Mae was the second oldest of five children. Two of her siblings, boys, one now in his forties, lived several miles away in a different town. The third and younger brother, who related this story, lived a few miles from her. Her youngest sister lived near New York and had a family of her own. Despite the relative peace in which their parents raised them, Mae's life would be punctuated with one failed relationship after another and a home that seems to house a malevolence that would later manifest itself.

After a brief marriage early in her thirties, Mae shortly

returned to the dating scene after discovering her husband dating the nurse who assisted him when one night he found himself in a car accident. Early in the marriage and during his recovery, Mae lavished her attention on him, showering him with expensive gifts on top of maintaining his lifestyle, which only she was responsible for. He remained unabashedly unemployed from their early years of dating up to their divorce.

Mae was like a mother figure, covering the mortgage on the stone house, the taxes and their bills. He, in turn, lived the lifestyle he had grown accustomed to, awakening late, having coffee and reading the paper cover to cover as she worked long hours as a fashion designer. It was months after his discharge from the hospital, on one extended weeklong trip to New York City, when Mae discovered the man who lived under her roof was having an affair with his former nurse.

Crushed and betrayed by the husband she doted on, Mae blamed herself for her long hours away from him. Instead of seeking a divorce, she apologized. Soon, the husband took advantage, asking for a "raise" in his allowance in order to go away on short jaunts to upstate New York with his paramour. As Mae's nerves began to fray from both the demands of her work schedule and the repeated clandestine meetings she would catch time and again, she began to sequester herself in the back of the house, overlooking the river. It was on one of those evenings, angry and emotionally exhausted, that she worried herself to sleep in the living room overlooking the backyard and the river beyond.

Mae awoke to the sound of flute music accompanied by what sounded like the strum of a harp. In the darkness, she slowly sat up and noted the late hour of half past midnight. She glanced out the open French doors to her patio and the gate beyond. Unable to shake the feeling of her deteriorating marriage, Mae walked out to the patio, and crossing the grass of the garden, she exited the iron gate and looked out at the river just a few feet from where she stood. She inhaled, hoping to calm her nerves, when a few minutes later she noted movement to her left.

Fearful of an intruder, Mae turned her attention to the left, where the ground receded to the river's edge. She backed away just in time to feel someone or something brush past her and dash for the river ahead.

A man in shadow, who appeared naked or clad in a skintight outfit, bolted into the river. She watched the fleeting glimpse of him as he disappeared into the river without a splash. It was as if he just entered it without disrupting the surface of the water. Terrified and feeling the hairs on her arms rise, Mae dashed back to the garden and shut the gate, latching it into place.

She crossed the garden and returned to the safety of the living room. As she looked out the French doors, she turned the lock and exhaled, surveying the quiet and dim living room. Upstairs, she heard the sound of creaking and reached for her cell phone to call her young brother, Paul. Minutes later, he came as she stood by the front door, sweating in fear. Police could find no trace of footprints in the garden or out by the river where she reported she'd seen the man bolt into the river. More than ever, Mae wished for a man who would love and protect her.

Despite the counsel of friends and siblings, Mae doggedly held on to her toxic marriage, blaming herself for the continued tryst. One day, now partially living with his paramour, the husband left without notice. Mae contacted the police, claiming her husband had met with misadventure and might be hurt. In less than two days, the "lost" husband was found. He filed for divorce, arrogantly accusing her of "meddling" in his affair when she should have known the marriage was over.

Just like the marriage Mae had, the ex-husband relied on the new woman for support. As soon as the divorce was final, Mae finally removed the man's name from the bank accounts they shared, and he started relying on the new woman for support. He reportedly remained unemployed with an alcohol problem when she last heard from him.

As the years went by, as if the marriage had been idyllic, Mae pined for her ex-husband, a man who remembered his birthday, not hers, and bought lavish gifts for himself on her credit cards. Mae justified his actions among her siblings as her own inability to be present in the marriage when he needed her to be home. Not two months later, unable to tolerate the silence in the house, Mae was once again sitting alone at clubs against the advice of her well-meaning friends.

Mae's former friends, women who had careers like her, who dressed and acted self-assured, were repelled by her behavior. Like them, she had been young once, and they understood her reckless, if not sometimes outspoken flirtations. They too knew how it was to be young and carefree, to dress provocatively time and again to attract the attention of suitors. However, Mae was now approaching her mid-forties. She had married late after bypassing all the men who had risen in their careers, financially stable, respected businessmen, lawyers and professors. Some had become artists in their own right, physicians and high-end sales representatives. In short, they were respected and now were entrenched in their own marriages, had started families a while back, and now lived at respectable addresses – some with alarm systems to keep the serenity of their "high end" address.

So had the majority of Mae's friends, who now worried about the growing crevasse of lifestyle differences between them and their lonely friend. They eventually all drifted away, repelled by her choices. However, one friend, "Cindy", remained loyal to Mae and was determined to help Mae find a "healthier" lifetime companion who would not take advantage of her.

Back to present day: Cindy, who also married late in life, felt for her friend Mae. As she planned one of her parties, she decided to invite Mae so she could introduce her to a local New York City artist whose works had been the topic in the past few years. "Peter" had had his own shows in the local galleries of Greenwich Village and one in East Berlin, Germany, in the past month. Now returned from his successful sojourn, Cindy decided to extend an invitation. Peter was a widower whose wife had succumbed to ovarian cancer and left him childless. Cindy felt that though it was too late for children, the two of them would form a bond, as they shared similar artistic professions, and the lack of children on both sides would strike a similarity of viewpoint as well as lifestyle.

Like Mae, Peter had a love of classical music, was liberal, if not far-right, and was well read and well traveled. Cindy hoped that his desire to tour places overseas would give Mae a fresh start and launch her out of the little sleeping town to reinvigorate a growing despondency in life. The question of how Mae, with her well-heeled upbringing, managed to attract men who had no love of books, travel nor art was a mystery among her friends. They saw little if not the total opposite of Mae in her choice of suitors and, finally, the man she had married, who turned out to be a drunk, lacking a work ethic, and was verbally abusive. Cindy, ever understanding and compassionate of her longtime friend, passed it off as "opposites attract", though she knew in the back of her mind that such marriages were doomed from the onset, as Paul put it in his narrative.

On the Saturday evening of Cindy's party, Mae appeared earlier than the other guests to Cindy's contemporary home not too far from her own further down the same river. Cindy knew Mae was trying a bit harder than what Mae now normally did, seeming more and more withdrawn and eccentric. Cindy was glad her friend had arrived earlier, as she saw this as a newfound energy for life. She hadn't seen Mae since that night she'd called her, frantic and highly emotional, claiming that her now ex-husband, Ron, had disappeared. As Mae entered and Cindy introduced her husband, Fred, Mae leaped into Fred's arms as if he had been a bosom buddy. Cindy was taken aback by the theatrics and so was Fred.

Paul leaned back, sipping his coffee as he paused for effect. His brows furrowed with worry as he recounted the evening's events. About a year ago, after his sister kept calling him on his cell with "distress" calls, he'd finally told her to stop calling him. He had had enough of bailing her then-husband out from barroom brawls, fights and jailhouse detentions for drunken driving. At some point, when he finally allowed his cell phone to ring, as his own business was being disrupted, his younger sister's husband started getting Mae's calls.

The "theatrics" would continue that evening as Mae became progressively more comfortable at Cindy's party. The man Cindy wanted Mae to meet finally arrived, albeit half an hour late, as he had been caught in New York traffic. It was at this point that Mae spent an hour in what Cindy hoped would be a charming conversation between the highly successful artist and her lonely friend.

As it happened, the artist friend brought along two others who lived locally in New York in one of the boroughs. One, an ad agency executive at one of the prominent companies based in midtown Manhattan, had a loft apartment, which had an area the artist rented from him as a studio. Adjacent to the studio lived the third guest, whom will be called "Ron".

He was five feet eleven with broad shoulders, blond hair and sparkling deep blue eyes; Ron's family was originally from a small village in the southern part of Sweden. In his early forties, Ron called himself a "perpetual bachelor" and "landed gentry" from Long Island. The artist would occasionally run into him in the hallway of the loft apartment, as Ron ran errands as a valet of sorts for the ad executive, who kept long hours in a high-pressure job.

Flamboyant in dress and extravagant in jewelry, Ron exuded an aura of a man who was used to luxuries. When they approached the small buffet table and the bar, Ron knew his wines well and tactlessly discussed a vintage that cost well over the wines that the other guests had brought to the party. Cindy rolled her eyes at Mae, to indicate it was "over the top" for a man who made his living as a valet to New York executives.

By the end of the evening, it was clear to Cindy that whereas the rapport that had been building in the early part of the party between Mae and the artist seemed to be gaining momentum, now it had fizzled out. Once again, to Cindy's consternation, Mae had walked out of the party, leaving the artist with a look of puzzlement and vexation.

34. MAE'S RIVER VISIT

As the party drew to a close, the artist took his leave, hastily departing before his executive friend and Ron, the valet, did. Cindy approached Mae in the foyer, whom at this point was freely helping herself to the remains of a vodka and tonic that Ron had given her. The two seemed to have hit it off and were now inebriated. Off they went out onto the patio and eventually ended up walking down the street and out of view of the house.

Cindy watched her friend disappear and turned to find the ad agency friend waiting for her. He smiled at her and indicated he was also departing very soon and to let the valet know that he should perhaps take the train or stay overnight in light of the number of drinks he'd consumed.

Cindy was appalled at Mae. She looked at the executive with reservation and asked about his valet. The man worked for him and, unknown to him, had a fondness for drink, as he'd witnessed that night. Perhaps it was because he'd met someone he seemed to have "clicked" with. Perhaps, Cindy said. She dared not let on that Mae was a longstanding friend. She was embarrassed and perturbed at Mae's behavior, though she reproached herself, knowing better from having observed in the past year or two that Mae had not been the Mae she knew from long ago.

Cindy, ever protective of her friend, wanted to know a little about Ron, who had walked out with Mae into the night. The exec indicated that all he knew was that Ron was very efficient with errands that he had hired him to do, such as groceries, dry cleaning and the occasional sweeping of his loft. No, he didn't think Ron was a bad character, merely that his job was mainly being a manservant and errand boy of sorts whom he'd met during the small gatherings of tenants in the building. Others also employed him, and he was reputed to be reliable and affable. Other than that, the ad executive did not know him.

Worried, Cindy tried to text Mae, but her cell remained silent. Cindy turned to her other guests, who still needed her attention. As the night progressed, she refilled their drinks, took note of food that needed replenishment, and rejoined what remained of the guests, being a consummate hostess.

Mae found herself in Ron's vintage VW Beetle, a relic that to her eyes seemed well maintained. In that she saw a man interested in history as he rattled on about his love of vintage cars, of which this was just one of many. He asked her for an impromptu tour of the area as his car perilously wove through the tiny streets of the river town. Once in a while, he caught a glimpse of the river that ran just a few yards from the road between the homes and trees that bordered both sides of the narrow road.

Suddenly, his condition still bordering being under the influence of the vodka, he turned the small vehicle onto a small street and aimed for the river. Even in Mae's state of inebriation, she noted that Ron had taken a turn that was a tad too sharp for her liking. Still, she giggled with excitement like a teen on a forbidden date, instead of a middle-aged woman who knew her driver was now over the alcohol safety limit. Now a few miles from her friend Cindy's house where they began, the drive had taken a perilous tone.

At the river's edge, perched just a few inches from the rocks below, Ron slammed on the brakes. Mae "awakened" from her stupor as her body was propelled forward by the momentum, with only the frayed seatbelt to hold her. She opened the door to the cold night breeze, the stiff chill hitting her immediately from the river, as the passenger side was adjacent to the edge.

As she turned to shut the door, she teetered at the edge – and slipped. A large hand grabbed her arm, and she heard a chuckle as Ron's powerful arm stayed her fall. Ever the romantic, Mae showered his action with compliments, laughing almost nervously. She would later recount this to her younger brother, who questioned her decision to leave the party in her drunken state, only to ride with a stranger. She later told Paul that Ron had originally proposed a "stroll" to ward off the intoxication they were both under.

Despite the chill and the precarious slope of the embankment, he tugged her like a child toward the rocks at the edge of the river. The swift current began to reveal itself as they edged closer. In the soporific state of intoxication that Mae found herself in, she came to a level of awareness that the currents were strong, and the wind was much colder than she expected. At that point, she asked him to help her back up the embankment, to the car and to return to the party.

He refused.

Mae's temper flared, feeling helpless like a child. She walked away from him, seeking a path where she could walk up the embankment herself. Ron yelled after her, telling her to watch her feet for rocks as she wound her way around the stones and rivulets with high heels, shoes she rarely wore.

Suddenly, she turned to discover he was right behind her, a scarf wound around both his wrists as if he was in the midst of placing it around her neck. She caught a look of anger in the otherwise jovial face. In a stern tone, he told her to follow him so they could ascend together, or he would tie the scarf around her neck like a dog on a leash.

Now intimidated, Mae followed his back while he wound his way up a path not familiar to her, and dimly she wondered how he knew about it if he was a stranger to the area. He was like a bad replay of the toxic and abusive marriage she'd once had. However, this memory would soon be replaced by her ascribing to him the traits of a "resourceful" man. Eventually, they reached the car, and Mae wordlessly reached for the passenger door – which was locked.

Ron leaped into the car like a young man in his twenties and revved up the motor of the old car. He looked through the passenger window and grinned. He reached and wound down the window and told her she was "no fun", then stepped on the gas, leaving Mae where she stood in the frigid air. In the dead of night, Mae walked back to the party dressed in high heels, her feet blistering when she arrived, to a surprised Cindy, whose guests had all departed.

Without a word and reluctant to share her foolhardy departure, Mae ignored Cindy's concerned questions. She refused her offer to drive her home, now clearly awake from the cold walk she'd had to do alone. Cindy counseled her to drive safely and told her friend that the executive hardly knew Ron.

Mae walked to her parked Volvo and drove away, unable to account for her perplexing evening. Her "radar" was too broken for her to realize the man she'd just met had just threatened her. Despite this encounter, Mae still somehow hoped she would see him again.

35. THE RIVER MAN

A few weeks rolled by uneventfully, but then Paul got a text from his sister again one evening. She was asking him to look at a car, which she indicated was in disrepair. Could he fix it? she asked. He texted back, indicating he was busy, but that he would try. Whose car was it? She replied it was "a friend's". She also then texted that she would pay him. Paul rolled his eyes, reluctant to become involved in one of his sister's activities, especially if it concerned another one of her male "friends".

Paul set a date for the following Sunday and shut the cell phone off, unable to force himself to wait for her reply. If that was when he was available, then that was that. He was not going to allow himself to be manipulated into working his busy schedule around her time. The week came to a close, and with that, Paul got another text, this time to come to the edge of the river where Mae indicated the said car was "stuck". She gave him the cross streets, and Paul clambered into his truck, now wondering with some guilt if he should have rearranged his schedule to see to the car sooner than he had been available. To his older sister, everything seemed to become an emergency, so

Paul had come to the conclusion, as their younger sister and brother-in-law had before Paul, that Mae tended to cry wolf just to increase the importance of her activities.

Paul arrived at the river's edge around four in the afternoon just as the last light of the winter sun had begun to fade. Mae was nowhere to be seen as Paul glanced down at his watch to note the time. He once more confirmed that the cross street was the correct one and then noticed an older model Volkswagen Beetle, which he recalled from Mae's last eventful evening based on her description. If it was the same car that was owned by the valet, then it didn't seem as well maintained as Mae had described the "vintage vehicle". It had a huge dent in the front fender.

As Paul approached, he heard Mae yell his name from somewhere close by. That was when he saw her sitting on a rock precariously close to the river water. His sister appeared worn out and agitated. Mae confirmed that the "broken" car was indeed Ron's Beetle. She then went on to say that it had been abandoned by its owner. After much questioning on Paul's part, here was Mae's story:

Mae had agreed to meet up again with Ron after the party from two weeks ago. He offered to drive down to her home and take her out to dinner. Despite the "small disagreement" they'd had after Cindy's party, when he'd left her to walk back in her heels alone, Mae chose to accept the invitation. Ron arrived on time at the appointed Saturday, the week before, and resumed their drive around the area as if nothing had happened. Mae never mentioned nor was she upset that her new acquaintance had left her stranded miles from Cindy's party. Instead, they carried on, with Mae continuing her consummate role as tour guide.

An hour after Ron had driven around the little town to survey its quaint streets, boutiques and parks, Mae gave him the directions to a small tavern on the New Jersey side of the river. He took her there for dinner, not forgetting to tactlessly mention that he would need to borrow cash from her in order to pay for their "date".

Paul recounted how the evening progressed from an amorous conversation to a volatile one: Mae's tastes, forever extravagant despite the fact that she was paying for the evening, went from a two-course dinner and dessert meal to one of lavishness. She ordered her favorite, oysters on the half-shell, in the small and intimate tavern with a view of the river and a white wine to match. She then ordered lobster and rib-eye, ordering for Ron the same thing. She ordered dessert for both of them, and then, refusing to end the evening so quickly, she ordered coffee.

By the time they left the restaurant, it was close to 10 p.m., and Ron drove her home, in what would be an interesting turn of events. Mae claims he professed his desire for her, body and soul with a "consuming fire" rivaling that of an eighteen-year old. Flattered, Mae invited him in to her Spartan but well-appointed home, where he saw she had the means with her taste in higher-end furnishings and original paintings – part of the ex-husband's anti-intellectual resentment that led to a bitter divorce.

Ron poured her scotch from the bar in the basement and started to become what reminded her of their first few hours after they'd left Cindy's home. This time, however, his advances were more determined in the seclusion of Mae's home. Mae's sense of propriety, loosened by the scotch, led instead to her tongue lashing out at his aggressive move to grope her. Still flirting despite her growing anger, she decided to go to the patio and around to where his car was parked.

Sliding in behind the wheel, Ron followed and shut the passenger door as Mae engaged the gear in a reckless manner, screeching the vintage vehicle out of the driveway and into the narrow street adjacent to the river. This time, as they drove, Mae decided to change his amorous advances by broaching the subject of a commitment, a trip to his flat in Manhattan, and a trip abroad in order to bring her closer to her fantasy of remarrying a man who had the financial means to uphold her lavish lifestyle. The valet, sensing his own financial inadequacy, lashed out a hurl of insults, accusing her of materialism and being a "user".

Cindy's house flashed by as Mae increased her pressure on the small car's pedal. This time it was Ron who saw his own life flash before his eyes as she pushed the car to its limits. Screeching to a halt right by the precipice of the river, they reenacted the previous tryst, this time Ron leaping out of the car in terror, anger and alarm mixed in his face.

Instead of exiting the car, Mae adjusted the gear in reverse, and backing up, aimed the vehicle at Ron. She stepped on the gas, and the car lunged toward the valet. He leaped out of the way in time, losing his footing and falling headlong towards the river.

It was at this point that Mae finally exited the car, grabbed a large rock, and proceeded to pummel the car's front fender with the rock, denting it. Ron lay unconscious, hitting his head below, as Mae stepped back into the vehicle and lunged toward a series of boulders that were meant to shield any individual from falling down below.

Slamming open the driver's door, she pulled the keys from the ignition and strode away, leaving Ron lying on the sand below. It was at this point that Mae once again walked home, passing a few pedestrians, who gaped in consternation at her wild appearance. When she got home, she texted Paul, requesting he fix the car she had just destroyed in a fit of anger.

As Mae sat seething in her bedroom, now dressed in her

nightgown, she stood to check the French doors and the front and back doors, locking and bolting them, suddenly afraid Ron might return. Her mental chaos becoming more and more pronounced, she willed herself to sleep.

An hour or so later, Mae woke up to a policeman in uniform at her door. At the front stoop was Ron, bedraggled with a red welt on his forehead. In shock, Mae feigned concern, excusing the event as a lovers' quarrel. The cop told her that Ron had told him Mae had destroyed his car and had attempted to kill him. Mae persuaded the cop that it was Ron who had tried to hurt her. After issuing a lecture to the effect that police do not get involved in domestic disputes, the cop asked Ron if he was pressing charges for the damages to his car. Mae ran into the house and offered her insurance card, stating that her brother would fix the damage at no cost to either carrier.

Ron turned to the exhausted cop and nodded his agreement and walked back out to the police car at the curb. The cop gave Mae a citation and indicated they would be filing a report about the incident. Mae picked up her cell phone and summoned Paul. Paul, in the midst of a busy and exhausting week, turned down his sister's request to fix the car that day. Instead, he agreed to stop and meet her the following week so she could lead him to the wreckage.

Night fell. Mae poured herself a glass of wine and then another, staring at a muted television. She fell into a slumber on her sofa with the French doors behind her, unlocked. A year later, as Paul recounted his sister's unstable frame of mind, he indicated Mae had always finished her stories of woe with a wish for a stable male "protector".

That night, the doorbell rang again. Mae bolted up in the darkened room and headed for the door, assuming Paul had changed his mind and had come to look at the car after all. She opened the door to find the porch empty. She stepped out and noted the streetlights were dimmer than usual.

Returning to the living room, she spotted a figure right outside the French doors. She slowly shut the front door behind her, latching it, apprehensive. Keeping her eyes locked onto the figure, she reached for a paperweight near a nearby lamp table and approached from the side of the sofa.

As Mae approached the figure, she noted with prickling familiarity the man who had leapt in the river before. She wondered if there was a man casing her home. She paused in time to see the figure turn its attention to her. It was completely in silhouette, and she sensed evil. The figure turned and disappeared.

Adamant to get a glimpse of the man's face, Mae dashed to the doors and opened them to the night air, heedless of her own safety. She stepped out onto the patio and felt something or someone watching her. She surveyed the backyard and stared out at the river beyond the gate to investigate. Nothing.

Mae stepped onto the grass and noted no footprints or depressions to show someone's feet. She thought it odd, as the man was very tall, though thin for his stature. She looked around in fear as her feelings of being watched intensified. She dashed back to her living room and shut the French doors, this time locking them. Then, in the corner of her eyes, she saw a wet area on her lamp table where she had picked up the paper-weight. It was wet with water as if someone had touched it with wet hands.

She looked down at her own hands still clutching the paper-weight. They were dry. She dropped the paperweight on the floor and noted that the carpet was soaked in water.

36. A BROTHER INTERVENES

Paul stared in consternation at his sister at a local diner. They had called someone in to tow Ron's car to his garage and decided to get a bite to eat so he could understand what had happened. He listened without judgment and wondered what was really happening at Mae's house. Part of him regretted not responding quicker, just in case there was an intruder at the house. Part of him wondered whether Ron had returned to Mae's home after leaving with the cop. It was all just too bizarre, this strange and explosive relationship. He wanted it to end for his sister's sanity as well as his own. Now he had the man's car in his garage, so he planned on quickly fixing the dent himself, as he was a collision specialist. This way, he could correct what Mae had done and return the car to its owner, whom he had never met, but felt he should in order to apologize on her behalf.

Who was the man outside the French doors? Was someone now stalking his sister, aware she lived alone? If so, was it one of her numerous "boyfriends"? As soon as Paul dropped Mae off at the house, he decided to call Cindy and tell her. She agreed to stop in with her husband to check on Mae later that evening.

Her husband knew the local police in the area, and they could arrange to have a few uniforms drive by to check the house periodically to deter a possible break-in. Mae had failed to note the name of the cop who had come to the door with Ron. She had misplaced the citation. Paul made a note to follow up with the precinct, as he wanted to resolve the car issue.

Then Paul contacted his older brother Glen, who invited him over to do some fishing. "Relax," he had told him. "You're handling it, and the police are already involved." Paul agreed to spend some time with his brother to get a break from Mae. His brother had just purchased a modest cabin in the Poconos, and Paul had not been to the cabin, a quick hour's drive from his condo. There, they could catch up and form a plan together to address their sister's dilemma.

As the week drew to a close, all was silent from Mae. Paul called the police and indicated that the car was in the shop, the paint dry, and ready for pickup. He followed up on the drive-by on his sister's house, and the police confirmed they would. Paul took a photo of the Beetle on his cell phone, evidence that Mae had done what she was asked to do to repair the damage she had done at his expense. He stopped by Mae's home and asked her to contact Ron to pick up the car and asked her to pay for the materials, minus his labor. A few minutes after he left her house, his cell rang. It was Mae again. She told him that Ron wanted her to pick him up in New York and take him to his car. Paul adamantly told her to stay away from Ron and arranged for an Uber to get the man in Brooklyn.

When a green Toyota Camry appeared at his garage later that day, Paul observed a nondescript man step out from the back seat. Paul described a man with beady eyes and a balding forehead emerge from the car. He was of average build with a paunch and not exactly how Mae had described the "dashing and dapper" date she had portrayed Ron to be. Without much introduction, the man approached the newly painted hood, touched it, and perfunctorily thanked Paul. Paul extended his hand to shake, but the man quietly ignored the gesture, entered the car, and left. *Rude*, Paul thought. Then again, his sister had asked for it.

Friday, Paul checked in on his sister and inspected the backyard in the afternoon sun. No footprints, as she'd reported. She had not seen anything since that evening. Paul exited the iron gate that led to the river and took in the beautiful view as the sun began its descent.

He spotted a mound of dirt, almost like mulch, by the edge of the river. Had he seen that before? Curious, Paul descended the slope leading to the river's edge. Whatever it was had a conical shape, too perfect for something natural. Just a few feet from him, he noted it was just slightly lower than his height of six feet. It was not mulch, but compacted dirt.

In the dimming light, Paul touched the edge with his foot and noted the firmness of the small antlike "hill". He decided it was recently formed, as grass had not grown on its surface. He kicked it and pulled back, wondering if he was disturbing a hornet's nest. A rather large one.

"It wasn't there before."

Paul leaped back in surprise, accidentally stepping on his sister's toe. She had emerged from the gate and was standing behind him the entire time.

"Did you recently get landscaping done?" he asked.

She shook her head, looking out at the river. Perhaps some anthill? Too large, he indicated. There were no ants on it or anywhere where a trail of ants would be.

Bees?

Mae returned to the house and minutes later emerged with a hornet spray. As he examined the mound, he realized that a hornet's nest would have had a hole or two detectable from the surface, and this one had none. He sprayed it anyway, noting that whatever lived in it would be back in its nest by now and inactive. Dimly, he wondered if snakes built hills like these. The thought made him instinctively move back a step.

He handed back the spray bottle to Mae and told her to expect a few cops in their cruisers passing by starting that night. She seemed relieved. Paul approached the mound, this time kicking it solidly with his foot for good measure. No snakes.

Part of the structure gave in, and the top collapsed like a mini-avalanche. May backed away as Paul watched, the spray aimed in ready for whatever emerged. Seconds passed. He shook his head and reentered the gate and bid her good night. Locking the French doors behind her, Mae waved at her brother as he left through the front door.

In the darkness, a man in silhouette stood by the front door as Paul left in his car. His eyes were luminous and red with anger. Mae turned to her left in time to see the man standing near her, exuding menace. She gasped as it made eye contact with her, and she backed away and slammed the door. Quickly, she parted the curtains on the side window near the door. No one was there.

The man had vanished.

Mae ran to the French doors leading to the backyard fronting the river and checked the locks. She looked out and saw the man "floating" past the gate, turning in the direction of the river. She blinked in disbelief.

Then she saw a flashlight searching her backyard. Mae looked through the front porch window and past the fence; she saw cops aiming their flashlights at her property. She opened the front door in relief to talk to them about the intruder.

As the two uniformed men walked the perimeter of the property, they noted no footprints and nothing amiss, other than the mound that Paul had examined and kicked earlier.

37. THE CABIN

Paul drove through wooded roads, which narrowed considerably as he entered denser forest above the small hamlet of Jonas, situated in a remote branch of state hunting grounds. His GPS had cut out as the vegetation thickened on both sides of his car. Suddenly, the road opened up to a small clearing, and the signal came clear again. He began to enter an unpaved road, which his brother had indicated would mark the road leading to his cabin.

Paul watched for signs in the dim light of one streetlight in the distance and switched his high beams on. Two lights from a porch light showed on his right, and he slowed, coasting the car into the drive of his brother's log cabin.

Rustic, isolated and calming was how Paul described the house. It had the mark of his brother Glen all over it. A hideaway well away from the stress of his brother's work at the township. As he slowed and parked, he thought about his sister in her cozy home and how her well-ordered house contrasted to the rusticity of the house ahead of him. No shrubs, no landscaping, no curbside lanterns. This one was more relaxed and less ordered in its calm.

Glen waved from the small side deck as Paul approached and noted with glad surprise that a stream ran on the side of the property. Glen was holding up another fishing rod with a grin that late Friday night.

"Told you I had a spare one just waiting."

Paul gave his older brother a knuckle shake, and Glen reacted with a hug. Paul grinned back as he examined the fishing rod and glanced at Glen's tackle box, open and brimming with lures of various colors and sizes.

He entered through the sliding glass door into an inviting cool living room with a large flat-screen TV showing the late news, a tower of DVDs and a brand-new sofa set and loungers. Nearby, he saw a kitchen with white pine cabinets stocked with plates and mugs. Glen opened the refrigerator and pulled out a six-pack of Stella Artois in bottles. *So unlike Glen*, he thought. As he moved to shut the door, Paul spotted steaks marinating in the coolness of the second shelf of the refrigerator.

They exited to the deck again, where they sat on Adirondack chairs to hatch their plan for the weekend. Paul wearily snapped open his first bottle of beer and kicked back. Around them, the sound of frogs and the susurrus of cicadas marked a summer night at its height. They were asleep by midnight.

By 9:30 a.m. the next day, they were deeply in the stream trolling for fish, Glen wearing his gaiters as Paul followed in cutoffs, the tackle box open on a large boulder. It was a perfect summer morning. Around noon they took a break for lunch, Paul cleaning the fish on the deck as Glen readied the marinated steaks on the grill by the railing below. He had brought large tomatoes and cucumbers from his wife's garden and was mixing the salad when Paul checked his cell phone for text messages. No message from anyone, including Mae.

Paul tossed the fish offal and scales on the ground below the deck and watched geese approach from the stream. Both men visibly relaxed as they sat down to lunch on grilled trout and steak, chuckling and enjoying their catch for the day.

As the afternoon wore on, Paul reclined at the edge of the stream and nodded off on the grass. Glen decided to wash off, and as he waded in, Paul recalled the profile of a man in shadow about twenty yards downstream on the opposite bank, in the shade of trees where the wood deepened. It was odd, he noticed, that the man wasn't fishing, but was just standing there looking out into the river. It appeared from his vantage point several yards away that the man wasn't even dressed in shorts or jeans or any type of fishing gear. But then again, he could only discern him in the shade, too dark to see details. Paul thought before he finally dozed off that he had told Glen there was another fisherman, but he wasn't sure he did.

Paul was startled awake at late dusk to find the wind had taken a chill. The trees were swaying, and the stream was moving faster than before. He sat up and pulled a sweatshirt he had bunched as a makeshift pillow under his head and stood to survey the area. He didn't see Glen, but saw that the man downstream was gone. He reached down for the tackle box, still open, and wondered if Glen had headed inside.

Pushing the sliding glass door aside, he spotted Glen sitting in the dark. His brother looked concerned.

"What's the matter? You okay?"

Glen looked up at Paul and told him that Mae had texted him to let him know that she had spotted police cruisers driving by and shining flashlights at her house. She had gone out and thanked them, inviting them in for dinner, but the cops refused.

"So, that was nice of her."

"Yeah," Glen replied, "but the cops reported she was inebriated and contacted Cindy about it." Cindy was now at Mae's house, making sure Mae was not drinking from her bar. Cindy had taken all the wine and hard liquor before she left, which made Mae angry at her friend. Paul shook his head in resignation.

"Nothing we can do about that," Paul exclaimed.

"We still need to think about getting help for her," Glen replied. Glen indicated that Cindy had quickly called to let him know that earlier that evening, Mae had told her that there was a man standing on the front porch, watching Paul as he drove off.

"Why didn't she call me to let me know?!" Paul exclaimed in exasperation.

Glen put both palms up in resignation.

They decided to go into the town, shoot some pool, have a late dinner of leftovers, and call it a night.

When the two brothers returned to the cabin later that night, Paul remembered to mention the "neighbor" he'd spotted down the stream. Families in the area usually had a cabin during the summer or came to rent for the summer. Glen looked back, perplexed, and said he'd have to drive around and see where the neighbors were located, as he did not know of any. No one had come to welcome them when they'd outfitted the house a few months ago. Maybe they were just people going through to check out the stream?

Meanwhile, back home, Mae awakened to a strange "whistle" outside her window. She sat up, noting the time was about half past 4 a.m. She wondered if it was a dream. She grabbed her robe and exited the bedroom, deciding to quickly recheck the locks on the front and kitchen door and the French doors to the patio.

She found the French doors unlocked. She looked out for anything amiss, surveyed the table and chairs to the side on the patio, and looked out at the gate. The gate was open.

Mae stepped back, trying to recall whether she or Cindy, during her friend's earlier visit that evening, had gone out to the patio. Perhaps it had been Cindy's husband getting fresh air or taking in the view of the river beyond. Mae inhaled in the stillness of the house and emerged onto the patio. She walked to the gate and stepped out. She noticed lights across the river. At the periphery of her view, she felt movement. She looked directly at the mound of dirt and observed something scratching the side of it. Slowly, she approached.

It was the man, dark as night, crouched at one corner of the mound. It wasn't dressed from what she could tell. Its back was to her as it attempted to rebuild what Paul had kicked. It was packing dirt onto the "hill" as if to try to bring it back to its former height. It paused as if it felt Mae watching a few yards away.

In awe and fright, Mae felt bolted to the spot as she watched the "man", whom she recognized was the same one who had noiselessly leaped into the river. When it paused, she felt the hairs on her arms prickle. She bolted for the gate, and that was when she heard an unearthly whistle once again. Then a "clock, clock" sound. She felt something pursuing her as the gate clanged shut and the bolt drove home. She tripped on the patio's raised edge, the "clock, clock" continuing behind her. She shut the French doors and turned the lock.

Mae quickly turned away and ran to the phone.

38. "MUMBO JUMBO" STRIKES AGAIN

E arlier in the book, I discussed an incident pertaining to Lisa's childhood home in San Juan, Philippines, where the family maid was feeding the cats in the backyard when she sighted a man dark as night hunched over – with gleaming red eyes. The incident in the previous chapter with Mae sounded similar, with the exception that the "man" this time didn't appear to be dressed in tatters.

In Mae's case, the disturbance of the "mound" earlier in the day seemed to have precipitated the sighting of the strange "man" twice in the space of a few days. It appears that by kicking it, Paul had disturbed whatever "rested" there. The existence of a "mound" of dirt is interesting, as the house in San Juan had a backyard that had a few "mounds" of dirt, which Lisa's grandmother had later discovered and forbidden anyone from touching. She had indicated to Lisa and her cousins that "elves" lived there and should not be disturbed, as they protected the plants and animals living in the backyard. To disturb the mounds was tantamount to bad luck or misfortune, according to legend. The mounds looked very similar to Paul's description, which he'd found by the river outside Mae's back wall. They were conical and packed without grass, as if just recently formed.

Back in the Poconos, Paul and Glen settled into the late afternoon after another full day of fishing. They once more resumed their roles: Paul cleaning the fish they caught, the guts and scales carelessly tossed over the deck and onto the grass. Glen made marinated steaks, which he once again tossed onto a hot grill. He added ears of corn for good measure and had a cold six-pack of Coors this time waiting for them in the refrigerator.

Paul watched a movie on Glen's DVD player, an old horror film from the '80s whose title he could not recall. He did, however, recall how drowsy Glen had become from the meal and from their beer. Glen begged off as soon as the movie was done and retired to bed in the loft. Paul chose to walk out onto the deck to take in some air and watch the stars, as the remote rural location made for a splendid view of the night sky.

As he slid the glass door open to walk out, he noticed a man right below the deck railing, picking up something on the grass. Alarmed at the intrusion, Paul yelled, "Hey!"

What Paul saw would forever seal in his head the horror movie he saw in real life: Not ten yards from him, the man in the dark straightened up and openly glared with huge luminous red eyes. It filled Paul with a sense of menace. It was the same one behind Mae's house just hours ago, flittering by the mound Paul had disturbed. A clopping noise ensued, like that of lizards landing on cement. Then a whistle. The figure stood about Paul's height of six feet two, though it seemed shorter since Paul was up on the deck, about to reenter the glass door when he caught it. Paul backed away in terror as the creature continued to glare back, holding his eyes. He had the presence of mind to slide the glass door shut and engage the lock.

Grabbing the security bar, he held it like a weapon, searching for something more threatening. He forgot his brother did not own a gun. The sound of the door slam roused Glen, who emerged from the loft and peered down.

"What's going on?"

Paul looked up and back at the deck, but the figure had disappeared. "There was something out there. A man."

Glen came running down, carrying a rifle Paul didn't know his brother had. He walked right past Paul and opened the door against Paul's advice.

Paul followed his brother and went down to the bottom of the deck where he had seen the man. All the fish entrails and scales were gone. He told Glen the figure looked like the man he had seen the other day facing the stream that late afternoon. Strangely, the man had no features besides the luminous red eyes, which told him it was from the netherworld. Glen did not believe in ghosts, but had no explanation.

The next day, the brothers left for home. Paul visited his sister to check on her, deciding on the way not to tell her about the strange man that he'd found outside the house. However, Mae told him with horror of her encounter with the man by the mound, and he listened, appalled at the similarity of her description. Troubled, Paul said nothing. As he was leaving, she asked him to feel free to have a cupcake or two, which she had baked earlier that day – and would he like to stay for dinner?

Not really big on desserts, Paul exited to the kitchen table, as he didn't want to offend his sister about her baking skills. After refusing dinner, as he had to catch up on what had happened at the garage in his absence, he exited to her small kitchen. He decided he would return later that night and sit outside to see if the "man" would return. Perhaps he could catch him, if he was a man, but the more he thought of the encounters, the more he began to think it was not a normal man, but some entity. He picked up a frosted cupcake and bit into it. He yelled out a

compliment as he exited through the side door of the house, still
chewing.

Out on the side porch, he almost stepped on what looked
like fish entrails and scales. He leaned down and confirmed, a
shiver running through him. He noted they belonged to a trout –
like the ones he'd scaled and gutted at his brother's cabin – and
had carelessly tossed on the ground. He straightened, now
feeling a sense of unease permeate his being. How did they get
here? He recalled how right after he and his brother came out to
confront the "man" outside the cabin, he had noticed someone
or something had cleaned up the entrails and scales he had left
there. Now they appeared to be in a cluster right on his sister's
back porch.

Paul's hairs on the back of his neck stood up. His brother had
not saved any fish for Mae, as she did not eat fish. He dashed for
the back garden and through the iron gate. The wind stiffly blew
past Paul as he eyed the mound a few yards away. He
approached and noted that the side he had kicked had been
repaired. It was back to its former shape. Then a "clock, clock-
ing" sound from somewhere near him could be heard. He
looked around in trepidation, the wind blowing cold as he
surveyed the surface of the river.

Paul never touched the mound of dirt again. Weeks passed,
and Mae's sightings of the mysterious man in silhouette ceased.

How did the mound of dirt end up in Mae's backyard? How
is it connected to the red-eyed "man" who exuded menace? Who
put the fish remains on her side porch?

39. THE FARMHOUSE AT THE EDGE
   OF THE FOREST

Along a narrow road at the very edge of a large state forest sits a large property. Bordered by the forest behind it and farmland on either side, an old stone eighteenth-century farmhouse faces a nondescript three-bedroom home with wood shingles, painted blue and white. From the outside, the smaller house looked like a rancher, with its living room windows and kitchen lined next to each other facing the road and the dining room and family room facing the expansive backyard and garage. The woman who lives in the blue and white home was in her early fifties at the time of the sightings. She no longer lives in the house after the singular events of 2012 that she witnessed in the farmhouse dwelling across the road.

"Leslie", as she prefers to be called, lived alone. Her husband, a long-distance truck driver, had left her and two children after a turbulent marriage that ended in divorce. Her two boys, then in their late teens, both joined the military and were both stationed abroad. Thus, Leslie lived alone through no fault of her own. The enforced solitude made her a choir member at a local church, an animal rescue helper, and an active member of a local book club.

Despite trying to keep busy at her job at a local IGA store and the volunteer activities, which afforded her some friend-ships, Leslie spent most evenings alone. Her only sister lived miles away in Florida, whereas Leslie lived in the cold climes of Upstate New York.

One late Friday evening, as Leslie returned from grocery shopping after an afternoon with the rescue shelter, she decided to spontaneously make coconut pudding. Leslie loved puddings but quickly grew tired of the usual supermarket offerings of chocolate, butterscotch and vanilla. She decided to experiment when she saw a few fresh coconut husks at the local grocery where she worked. The manager was practically giving it away, as few people in her area cared for unsweetened coconut in its natural state, still in its husk. So off she went to grab some flan pudding from the shelf to improvise a new dessert.

As Leslie stood by the sink, struggling to open the husk with a large butcher knife and mallet, she glanced out the kitchen window, which faced the lone farmhouse across the street. Set back further in the yard than her own home, the farmer and his wife lived with two setters and a cat to make up for a childless marriage. Tonight, she noticed the farmer open the front door to let out the dogs and even the cat, who strode up the path towards the road.

Frustrated with the husk, which wouldn't break open, she wondered if she should place it on the chopping block in the backyard where she split wood. She exited her kitchen through the back door as she heard the two dogs barking furiously. There must be a fox or deer nearby, she surmised.

The screen door slammed shut as Leslie placed the coconut on the large wood block, searching for the axe she had left lying somewhere. The dogs seemed to be in a frenzy now. Curious,

Leslie turned, walked to the side of the house, and saw a bear on its hind legs by the edge of the field, running away.

Leslie looked around her, concerned another one was nearby, but across the street the farmer emerged with his shotgun as the creature ran for cover. The elderly man, still robust with a shock of silver hair, turned and waved at Leslie when he spotted her. She waved back with a smile.

Leslie found the axe lying by the side of the house and, grabbing it, proceeded to hack at the husk. It opened, juice flowing out, to her surprise. Leslie grabbed the two halves and then, for self-protection, turned back and grabbed the axe before going inside.

She made her pudding and made a mental note to separate some to offer the farmer and his wife. No harm offering, she thought. If they don't care for it, they can toss it. The couple had been born and bred in the area and were strictly meat and potatoes. She felt their isolation as much as her own and wanted to continue reaching out in friendship.

As night settled in, Leslie went about her routine of poring through countless DVDs her sons Ron and Steve had downloaded and brought along the last time they were there for dinner. They knew she loved movies and prepared for their being away by making sure she was occupied. She looked forward to their calls once a week, though at times she felt they were rushed and needed to hang up immediately. She worried about them endlessly though they were coming into their early twenties. In her mind, they would always be her little boys.

Leslie settled on the sofa, clicking remotes as she turned on the electronics her sons had set up for her. Though she was in the middle of nowhere, with the town about four miles down the road and the next neighbor besides the farm another mile or two, she felt connected with her flat-screen TV and satellite dish. Both had been Christmas presents from her sons. On a lark, the assistant manager at the IGA had given her his used DVD player after getting a more recent brand. She felt fortunate that way.

Leslie shut the lights off, settling on a suspense film from the '60s. She recognized the actors and became quickly absorbed as the night wore on. She threw a popcorn bag into the microwave. The pop-popping began in a few minutes.

Minutes later, the microwave dinged to announce the popcorn was done. But then the popping continued somewhere, it seemed, outside the house. Leslie muted the sound on the TV and listened. It was definitely coming from somewhere near the kitchen. Outside her house.

Leslie walked over to the microwave and took out the steaming bag, listening. Pop, pop. Pop, pop.

She edged closer to the kitchen door she had shut earlier and engaged the bolt. She parted the curtain and peered.

Pop, pop.

Leslie touched the wall near the kitchen door... and waited.

Pop, pop, pop, pop!

Leslie backed away after feeling the vibration with the palm of her hand – on the wall! Whatever was making the noise was rapping on the wooden shingle outside.

Crap, Leslie thought. *I have a woodpecker*. She wondered if the bird was destroying her siding. Leslie turned the light on the kitchen porch, unbolted the door, and emerged.

She will never forget the next few seconds.

In the darkness around the small glow of the porch light, she sense a presence hold its breath. Then an exhale. A smell assailed her nostrils, like something rotting.

Silence.

In terror, Leslie backed in and shut the door, hurriedly bolting it again. She moved the curtains on the door so it obliterated her view of whatever was outside. No, that was not a woodpecker.

She gasped for breath, not realizing she was also holding her breath the entire time. She wondered if she should call the police. What would they do? Did the bear return?

Forever afraid of crying wolf, Leslie decided to recheck all her windows and the front door. She looked out through her picture window in the living room and saw nothing except the sole lamp light from the end of her driveway. She told herself she needed to get motion lights for the backyard and perhaps a stronger porch light for the front entrance.

The popping sound had stopped.

Leslie sat in the dark, deliberating on calling the police, a small crew of men who hardly saw violence in the little town. She decided to forgo it and instead pay a visit to the couple in the farmhouse the next morning. She didn't want to raise the alarm and forever be seen as the "paranoid woman" who lives alone. The coconut pudding was a good idea. She would bring that in and mention what she'd encountered tonight.

Perhaps they could tell her what it was. Perhaps. For several years since she got married, Leslie had lived in the house. It was a modest home, meant for couples just starting out. It was further away from the neighborhoods, even after the construction started on the large homes they called "McDonald Land" homes. Homes where the sizes of the garage were as large as her home. She was glad they had chosen to live near the farm and away from town. Recently, development had also encroached on the woods to her right a few miles away, which were totally wild and unpreserved. These homes were even larger than the other development, with huge glass windows, towering fireplaces, and decks that seem to fit more than two dozen people.

Leslie unmuted the TV and resumed watching her movie. It was a suspense film about a woman who was jogging alone in the middle of the night. She stopped and ejected it and opted for a comedy.

L eslie awakened from a deep sleep to find that it was already close to 9 a.m. She was glad it was a Saturday, and it was her day off from the grocery store. She leapt into the shower, dressed, and made coffee, opening the refrigerator to take out the coconut pudding. She looked at the phone and tried to remember if Mr. and Mrs. Taylor, the sole neighbors across the street, were on her speed dial. She glanced out the kitchen window and decided they were home and, as farmers go, would be up at this hour. Nine a.m. is considered a late start in farming families. No need to call.

Leslie covered the bowl of pudding in shrink-wrap, leaving half for herself for tonight's dessert. She took one glance at the farmhouse across the street, ran her fingers through her short bob, and walked out through the front door.

The doorbell was an old-fashioned wind chime with brass bells. Mrs. Taylor, a woman in her early sixties, opened the door with a warm smile.

"Well, look who's here, Jim!"

Leslie offered the pudding as Mrs. Taylor invited her into the spacious home with wood beams on the ceiling. Leslie had been there a few times in the past few months and was always a bit surprised at the character of the house. The couple chatted and talked about the upcoming harvests and the fruit trees on the property, offering Leslie some of the harvest. At length, Leslie thought it was appropriate to bring up last night's strange event.

"Do you have problems with woodpeckers lately?"

Mrs. Taylor turned to her husband, who shook his head, but Jim was obviously curious.

"Was there damage to your house?"

Leslie thought for a moment and made a mental note to check by her back door. "I'd have to check... but..."

"Yes?"

"I don't know... about nine or ten last night, I was watching a movie..."

She told them the strange popping sound she'd heard by her back door right after the popcorn was done popping.

The Taylors darted a look at each other, and Mrs. Taylor looked down. Jim signaled her to continue.

"So I looked out the door and finally opened it –"

"And?"

"– and there was just this terrible smell... not like a skunk... but it smelled like really bad BO. Almost like a homeless man was out there..."

The couple leaned back, visibly shaken.

Lena, the wife, ventured, "How did it make you feel?"

Leslie thought it was a strange question to ask, but she replied, "I – I thought it was the bear – again."

Jim's eyes widened. "You saw that creature by the side of my house yesterday!"

Leslie nodded. "Yes. I went back for my axe and saw you shoo it away with your gun."

Jim warmed to the theme. "I remember you waved at me."

"Yes. I saw it run back to the woods."

"Say that again, Leslie?!"

"It ran into the woods."

Jim qualified: "You mean 'ambled', right?"

Leslie hesitated, recalling what she'd seen.

Her jaw dropped. "It ran, Mr. Taylor."

Jim and Lena Taylor looked at each other and nodded.

Lena reached over and touched Leslie's hand in reassurance. "We saw THAT too."

"What do you mean?"

Jim looked back at Leslie. "Hon, bears don't RUN. They amble."

Leslie glanced back and forth at the couple. "So, it was a man? Are you saying..."

"We don't know what it is, do we, Lena? But it's definitely not a bear. At least not the one we saw yesterday morning. Whatever it was ran on two feet. Not on all fours."

The Taylors invited Leslie to stay for an early lunch, and she accepted. Part of her did not want to be alone in the house across the street after the discussion. Who knows what would emerge from the woods behind her house. Mr. Taylor sensed she was reluctant to leave and volunteered to take a look at the "scratches", if any, by her kitchen door. Perhaps, for her it was a wild animal such as a raccoon, anxious for leftovers she might have left in the kitchen stoop. He offered the explanation to calm her, she thought.

Mr. Taylor exited their kitchen, strode across the wide expanse of grass, and escorted Leslie to the side of the farmhouse, where he showed her scratches made by a raccoon on a pile of logs leaning against an old outhouse that had gone to disuse. He told her she was welcome to the logs this winter should she need them, but to keep them away from the house's siding, as they could gather termites. Leslie thanked the old farmer, his arms weathered but sinewy for a man his age. He pointed to the horses several yards away in the barn.

"See my mares?"

"Yes."

"They love to roam the paddock. But when they feel threatened, they neigh, stomp their feet, and run for the barn. So I keep the stalls open for them."

"Did that 'bear' or whatever it was upset them?"

The man nodded. "Yes. You want to keep an ear out for them, as they will signal you when there's something afoot. I had a third dog here one time. An Irish setter too. Chloe." The man looked like he was about to cry.

Leslie wanted to ask the next obvious question.

"We'll talk about that another time."

Jim ambled over to Leslie's house and examined where she thought the popping sound had come from. He looked at the cedar siding and observed nothing. He leaned down, looking at the bent grass.

"I don't mean to alarm you or nothing – but something WAS here."

He pointed to the bent grass. Whatever it was, was bipedal.

Jim put his foot over one.

"I got size 10 feet." He looked at Leslie, who looked back in surprise.

"A man taller than you."

He stepped on top of the other print. "Much, much taller."

"Oh, my God."

"Listen for my horses. If you hear them, look out and call me."

"Should I call the police?"

Jim hesitated, almost to the road, and turned around. "You could try."

"Have you reported it before? Seen it before?"

Jim sighed, arms akimbo. "Lemme put it this way: I hear people talk about this in town. I never saw anyone or anything like that, but it was no bear. I've seen bear. I've seen wolves. When they DID report them, nobody could catch whoever or whatever it was."

"Is it dangerous?"

"I don't know. As long as they run when we show up, we're good."

But in Leslie's recollection, whatever it was at her back door DIDN'T run when SHE showed up. It had been out there and she'd heard its breath. Foul.

41. MOTION LIGHTS

A stiff wind blew as the man stepped down from the ladder, wiping his hands on his paint-stained jeans, worn from use. He looked up at his handiwork at the edge of the house where the roof met the corner of the siding. Leslie joined him, looking at the two motion lights. One light pointed west, the other north. They walked over to the other end of the house where the meadow continued to undulate into the distance.

They stopped to look at the other lights, identical to the first, one pointed south, the other pointed east. The man touched the cord, which he had pressed and stapled to the edge of the siding and where a hole had been made going into the house.

"So you should be good as far as backyard lighting. This power cord is plugged into the kitchen socket, but don't turn the switch off, or it won't work," the man explained.

"Great. Hopefully it never goes off."

The man glanced at Leslie. "Well, it'll go on even if it's just you or your neighbor there."

"Yeah. I understand."

"And you just want a lamppost up front to match the other?"

"Is that cheaper?"

"I can make it cheaper if you'd like. Doesn't have to be anything fancy if you don't mind a wooden pole and the light just being simple. Like the other one."

"Please. I just need the light."

The man surveyed the surroundings, noting the meadow and the woods behind the farmhouse across the street. "It must get awfully dark at night."

"It does."

Leslie chose not to volunteer any information to the stranger. He had been referred to her by a coworker at IGA, and she wanted to leave it at that.

He sighed and prepared to leave, putting his cap back on.

"Well, ma'am, I will get to it and give you a call when I get the post together. I imagine sometime next week." He took out a cell phone and snapped a photo of the light post.

"Can you try sooner?"

The man glanced back, lifting his glasses. He was in his mid-forties, sinewy, with an open face and a look of genuine concern. "Someone coming up to the house? Did you have a prowler?"

Leslie sighed, reluctant to share more. "Not quite a prowler..."

The man sighed and leaned on one leg. "Listen. I'm always out on these jobs, and I got two teenagers who are hardly home on weekends. Even weeknights, once they started to date... You know what I mean. So my wife's alone most of the time, and she's got this leg injury..."

"I'm sorry..."

"What I'm saying is, we live just a few miles from here, so I just wanna rest my mind a bit as I..."

"Then you understand my predicament with your wife alone and all."

The man nodded vigorously.

Leslie rested on one leg and decided to tell. "Well, in that case... I'll tell you what I saw and what I smelled over there..."

A few days later, the man was back and had an assembled light post in the back of his truck. To Leslie's surprise, he told her his wife had also had an unexplainable encounter while walking one night with their dog. Something had crossed her path, just a few yards ahead, walking on two legs. She'd smelled something like a dead corpse before she saw what she thought was a gorilla cross their path. Their German shepherd had been so terrified it was slinking around her legs, and she almost fell. The man's wife had turned around and dashed back to the house, the dog practically running ahead of her and dragging her to go faster.

42. THE OLD APARTMENT IN FRANCE

Tucked into the Mediterranean coast at the southern border where the French and Italian border sits, are the charming villages and towns that cluster around the city of Nice. Sunshine and tourist attractions permeate the area, as the region hums with culinary delights, the beauty of historical architecture and the promise of good wine. Replete with culture, refined and heady with pride, the Nicoise people cater to over 100,000 tourists every year from every corner of the globe.

Due to the influx of both tourists and expats alike, the villages and Nice in particular are punctuated by villas for rent, called "gites" in French. Some are more well-appointed than others, and some are humble apartments for tourists and visitors on a budget – in every area of Nice.

One corner of Nice, hugging the shoreline near the historic port, is "Vielle Ville" or Old Town. This triangle-shaped area was architecturally preserved for its charming and unique look of yesteryear. Vielle Ville, save for some main roads, has narrow pedestrian streets. Its streets spoke of an unhurried past when people worked to live, eating their meals and savoring them in a leisurely fashion, watching people go by and socializing with each other without cell phones or electronic interference.

Even today, that culture of a life made simple and full of quality pursuits in gardening, quality cuisine, great wine, arts and festivals still permeates the region. Most expats hope to capture the lifestyle and were coming in record numbers. Within streets are clustered dwellings, mostly old and renovated to accommodate restaurants, bars, patisseries, boulangeries, poissoneries and, of course, apartments for both residents and expats. Some are rented out to tourists so that every flat is always inevitably occupied from week to week and month to month.

One of these apartments is situated in an ideal location where it was centrally located within reach of the shopping district, the restaurants and the local tram and bus. The apartment was a one-bedroom with a full kitchen, modernized for conveniences with even a washer and dryer adjacent to the full bath. The windows faced the busy street below, and the outer façade was as quaint and old as the rest of the old town: real shutters, which functioned for both privacy and noise reduction, and real plants lined the ledge outside.

It was in this apartment that a couple and a small child decided to rent for two weeks in order to leisurely partake of the energy of the Riviera. Janine and Mark flew in from the Swansea area of the UK with their six-year old daughter, Emma. Their intention was to explore the region and decide on whether it was a good place to live. Invited by some friends who lived in nearby Vence, a village located twenty minutes away, they decided to stay in an apartment in Nice, as their friends both worked during the day, and they did not want to be an inconvenience.

Janine wanted to make contact with the local embassy before leaving, but decided that they should keep it a holiday and just get first impressions, keeping their eyes open for what it offered to children of Emma's age. Emma sang in her school's first-grade choir and had a beautiful voice. Janine wanted to cultivate the child's talent and expose her to culture at an early age. This was that holiday.

Mark scheduled trips to the surrounding villages to see art galleries, museums and noted concert offerings of a classical and vocal nature. The village of Saint Paul de Vence, a gallery of artists in its streets, was only two miles from Vence where their friends lived. The friends decided to have the couple stay overnight at the end of their stay, visiting the galleries in the neighboring town before they took them to the airport for the flight home.

As much as Mark wanted to attend classical concerts and vocal performances for his Emma to see, his timing was far from perfect, as the two weeks did not really have many events that would allow them to see an open-air classical concert or opera in the vicinity. It was a disappointment, but it was part of the reason why Mark wanted to leave his position and seek to start his own business. It would allow him to dictate, as best he could, when he could take his little family on vacation. He reasoned that if he had his own business, the timing would include tickets to the plays, music festivals and even operas in the area.

Although the music part of the trip was a letdown, the couple did not allow this to dampen their spirits. They still scheduled several escorted day trips to the villages, including Monaco, Tourettes Sur Loup and Eze, where they could all take in the art, architecture and culinary delights of the region. Mark loved wine and so did Janine. He hoped that on this trip his daughter could be exposed to wine as a dinner item so that her tastes in young adulthood would already be refined and culti-vated. Some of Mark's friends thought it might make the child a "snob", but Mark said perception was part of the perceiver, not the person. He would raise her to be humble and down to earth, knowing that all rewards came from hard work. Whatever others chose to see was none of her business. He would raise her to be self-confident and comfortable within her own skin.

Mark and Janine were both fun-loving, and it wasn't lost to them that in order to educate their young daughter, it had to be fun. Janine had dreaded her piano and ballet lessons as a child, not knowing what it was aimed to do, until much later she actually saw a ballet performance. This time, she would not make that mistake and expose her own child to performances and have her decide on her own what she would like to try if she stopped singing for fun.

So they began their trip in earnest from day two, sleeping in to help the small child catch up on sleep after a three-hour flight, but starting early the very next day to help their internal clocks readjust. They sipped café with crème in demitasses, took a tram tour with the rest of the tourists, pointing out the public park with fountains as a later visit after lunch, then going to Finocchio's for ice cream. Janine ordered ice cream made from violet flowers, which encouraged Emma to try the flavor. They walked the promenade by evening, waiting for the seven p.m. meal at a nearby seafood restaurant to open.

By 9 p.m., Emma was nodding off. Mark carried their daughter up the steps to the first-floor flat and watched her sleep. Then they rolled in to the bed next door in front of the flat-screen TV and picked out a DVD from the landlord's large collection reserved for his tenants. Outside, the dim susurrus of holidaymakers could be heard as they milled about and dined in the open cafés a floor below.

A week went by. The small family settled into a routine, with Mark awakening early to run a few miles on the promenade by the beach, just eight short blocks away. He stopped to grab coffee and pastries on his way back and set the small bistro table on the balcony with steaming coffee and pastries. He poured a glass of fresh pear juice for Emma and read the French paper as best he could to catch up on local events. Below him, the silent street returned to life at 7 a.m. to resume commerce. When the rest of the family awakened, they prepared for the next tour and planned for a new restaurant on their return. It was becoming a heady habit, which Mark hoped would become a lifestyle when he retired.

At the beginning of the second week, the family took an excursion to the beach resort of Antibes, a pricey locale further down the coast. This time they took the unreliable public transport and didn't return to the area until well after the dinner hour. At that point, Emma began to fret, so they quickly headed for a local pizzeria, encouraging her to keep awake for the short walk back to the apartment.

Temporarily disoriented, Mark looked at the streets, surveying the small plaza, which was his signal to turn left onto the small pedestrian alley that meandered to their apartment. He found it and tugged at Emma, who sleepily held her father's hand with a belly full of pizza. They would have to watch TV in order to digest before calling it a night.

Janine was following behind her husband and daughter when they finally entered their pedestrian street, which was filled with tourists strolling and dining. She looked up to locate the apartment's distinctive balcony, where she had left a dish-towel to dry over the railing.

Her eyes made contact with a woman with blonde hair looking out through the balcony's shutters, which they had kept open to air out the apartment. Janine paused, taken aback. She decided it might not be their apartment, but looked at the restaurant beneath to determine the location. It was the same restaurant.

Janine touched Mark's sleeve and pointed up. The woman

had a shadowy dress of some type in dark blue, with a frilly neckline.

Mark looked up and then looked back at Janine. Janine looked again as she pointed, but there was no one there.

"What was it?"

"I could've sworn there was a woman looking out the window of our balcony... almost like she was about to step out."

Mark paused, looking up, holding the keys to the front door leading to the building. "We'll see in the few minutes. Maybe the landlady is paying us a quick unexpected visit."

The little family unlocked the door to the apartment and entered. Immediately, they smelled something akin to verbena.

"You smell that, or is it just me?" Janine's eyes were luminous.

"Come on! You're just tired. The landlady probably came in and sprayed some air freshener. Good thing, as we were airing it out anyway."

Janine kept looking around and finally approached the balcony and looked down. She turned and jumped, not expecting Mark to be right behind her.

He kissed her on the cheek. "Hey, I'm here."

Janine sighed and relaxed. "Glad you are!"

43. MIDNIGHT

By 12 p.m., Emma was fast asleep on the foldaway couch. Mark shut the bedroom door, and as soon as his head hit the pillow, he fell into a deep sleep. Janine lay awake, staring at the shutters of the bedroom window, where the streetlight filtered through. She rose and decided to shut it and hoped that by doing so, the room would become darker and allow her to sleep. She was overtired, wound up from the day's events, and the lady at the balcony had an anxious, almost scared look upon her face. She knew what she was seeing and the feeling she got as she was watching the lady was terror.

Janine opened the double-paned windows and felt the breeze from the night air waft in. Down beneath her, pedestrians walked, some hand in hand, some in groups, laughing. Glasses and silverware still tinkled from late-evening diners. She marveled at the lateness of the dinner hour. She reached for the shutters, touching the well-constructed wrought-iron closure. The sounds muted as she shut it and closed the glass windows. No sound from the street could now be heard.

Janine lay down and finally slept.

Janine awakened dimly to chimes. She was in a twilight

slumber, not fully awake, but she thought she heard a woman singing. The voice was beautiful and sang in some foreign language. It did not seem to be in French. In the background music, the most beautiful notes from what seemed like a flute and harpsichord issued forth. She thought there must have been a neighbor across the way who was up early and singing. She felt lulled by the music and once again fell asleep.

"How did you sleep last night?" Mark was sipping coffee on the balcony as their daughter ate a raspberry croissant. Janine looked across the way at the neighbor's balcony.

"Great. I was treated to a concert."

"Really!"

"Yup. I think we have a musical neighbor." Janine pointed with her cup to the balcony across the way, the shutters closed.

Mark looked over. The shutters were closed, the plants on the balcony dead. "Not much of a gardener, I'm afraid."

"No, but we were looking for a concert, remember? They may know."

"It's an idea. Are you suggesting we knock on their door?"

"Why not?"

Mark leaned back and shrugged. "Let's ask the restaurant downstairs if they know of any before we do that to a local we've never met. I don't want them to think we were being nosy."

"Fair enough. They may even know who lives there."

"True."

"I'll ask."

"Okay."

"Beach day today?"

"Sure. I have to go to the market this morning, though."

"Of course. Flat peaches and wild strawberries..."

"... and ice cream with pistachios!" Emma volunteered.

Mark laughed. "And pistachio ice cream! How can we forget!"

Mark gave Emma a high five.

Marked glanced at his wife, pensive. "Any more ladies at the balcony? This balcony."

Janine shot back a dirty look at her husband. "Stop. You're giving me the jitters."

"Are we getting a balcony like this, Mummy?"

44. THE NEIGHBOR

The couple took Emma to the park, who played in the water fountains in her little frilled bathing suit. She joined the other children, and the couple almost lost her in the group of children who seemed to wear identical bathing suits. They lunched at a sidewalk café off Place Rossetti and pondered on taking a walk to the port side of Nice. But Janine's sighting of the woman on their balcony bothered her. As soon as lunch was over, Janine walked back to their alley and homed in on the door across from their flat. It appeared that there was a similar entranceway.

As Janine was about to knock, the restaurant owner emerged from across the street and asked if she needed help. She was glad he spoke English, as most of the people in the area did.

"I would like to talk to the lady upstairs. We heard her singing last night."

"Upstairs?"

"Yes, up there?" Janine pointed to the balcony across from their flat.

The man looked back, amused. "I'm sorry. My brother and I live there with my mother. But she is not a singer."

"Oh."

"We own from here to here." He pointed from one end of the building to the adjacent alley.

"Do you know if any of the tenants in our building sing? I know I heard it last night. We just want to have our daughter hear her if she performs. Maybe somewhere here in Nice?"

The man looked back, puzzled. "What time did you hear her? We have some musicians here in the restaurant if you like music. Jazz."

Mark joined the conversation and ventured, "Sorry, but my wife said it was operatic... with some type of harp or harpsichord?"

The man smiled, shaking his head. "I don't know about classical. We do not know anyone here in this area for that. My restaurant has local jazz musicians... sometimes we have someone play old Beatles tunes, you know."

Janine mused.

"However, you can check the local paper for musical events coming up... there are festivals later in July as well..."

"So, I think I will check with the neighbor next to us..."

Mark nudged her. Janine shot him a dirty look. It was not lost on the restaurateur.

"Hmmm... what I can do is ask my mother if she knows anyone in the neighborhood who sings opera... or something classical? She's lived here all her life." The man winked.

"Sounds good." Mark winked back.

"How old is your mom?" Janine ventured.

"She's in her eighties. She is still healthy. You are on the first floor, yes?" He looked up at their balcony.

Janine nodded. "We should be home tonight. I am planning on cooking."

The man smiled. "Please. Don't trouble yourself. Come to my restaurant. I will ask my mother to come down if you don't mind her joining you for dessert. Our food is authentic and so is the dessert. On us, of course."

Mark and Janine looked at each other. "Are you sure?" said Mark.

"We don't want to impose, but..." Janine was interested.

"*Pas de probleme.* It is our pleasure. *S'il vous plait.* 19:30?"

Mark nodded. "Yes, please. Thanks so much."

"*Avec plaisir, Monsieur...*"

"Please, call us Mark and Janine. This is our daughter, Emma. We are from Swansea, originally, but we live in Midhurst. In England."

A man in a waiter's uniform emerged and summoned the owner.

"*Girard Malpais.*" He shook Mark's hand, waved and rushed to the waiter's summons.

A petite lady, well-dressed in linen with her silver hair in a bun, joined the couple later that evening. Mark pulled a chair for her as Gerard, the restaurateur, introduced his mother.

"My English is *un peu*, but I can listen."

Janine smiled warmly. "Thank you for joining us. We are glad to meet you."

"I want to let you know that I have lived here all my life... I used to know everyone in this area, but now... so busy."

Janine nodded, urging her to continue.

"So many tourists, so many from England and *Etats Unis*, yes?"

"Yes, we are looking perhaps to live here."

The woman gave them a look of surprise and smiled. "France has much to offer old and young."

Janine ventured: "Yes, speaking of which, we would love to find out if there are any classical concerts... perhaps vocal performances. Emma has a beautiful voice, and we want to expose her to the music performances here."

"My wife heard a woman singing in the middle of the night and thought it was you."

The elderly woman glanced back at Mark and turned serious. "You heard music from your apartment?"

"*Oui.* Just the night or early morning before."

"What time, please? Do you know?"

Janine leaned back. "It was very early morning. I usually get up at six... Emma was still asleep. I heard a beautiful woman's voice... like opera... and there was music. Harp or harpsichord music in the background."

"You told me around 2 or 3 a.m.," Mark offered.

The elderly woman nodded gravely. She leaned back in her chair and reached for her Kir Royale, a wine mixed with champagne. She sipped, lost in thought.

"No one on this street or even the next sing opera or any classical music. No one I know here owns a harp or harpsichord. In olden times, the flute used to accompany the harpsichord. Or the piano."

Janine shot her a look of recognition. "That's it. It was flute with a harpsichord. Yes. Definitely."

"*En Francais?* In French?"

"No, more like..."

"Perhaps Italian?"

"Sort of."

"Are you aware the original settlers were Italian? Before the port was built? Then Nissart. The language of French and Italian sort of mixed together. This became part of France later on."

"Nissart is a language?"

"*Oui.* Like the meal my son prepared for you is Nicoise, but the language spoken was called 'Nissart'. Look at the street signs – the second from top on the corner of buildings... See?"

Janine and Mark followed where the lady's finger was

pointed, on the edge of the building near them. Two street names.

The elderly lady looked up at her apartment. "I have old records... If you would like to come up tonight... I will play Nicoise music for you – in the language of Nissart."

"Is it still performed now? Somewhere in the area? She may be singing in Nissart, and I'd like to hear her."

"Come up now if you're done. I will be glad to put it on for you."

Up the stairs they went and into a warm, inviting apartment furnished in brocades of light blue and white. The walls were wallpapered, and the scent of lavender and musk filled the air.

It was more like an old Frenchwoman's flat rather than two brothers who shared it with their mother. It was the woman's original home where she and her now deceased husband had raised their two sons. The sons had inherited the business started by their father. They never left the area.

With a flourish, the elderly lady reached for a record within a clean mahogany bookcase set on one wall filled with filigree ballet dancers. She collected figurines from Limoges, a town situated near the other end of France.

"Here is one from the area. As a matter of fact, she lived in this neighborhood."

The record played and filled the apartment with music.

Janine sat down, recognizing the woman's voice and the melody in the background.

"Do you hear the flute and harpsichord?" ventured the elderly lady.

"Yes. I believe that's her!"

Mark looked back at his wife, astonished.

He looked at the elderly lady. "Can we see her perform?"

"You mean NOW?"

"Yes."

"I'm afraid not."

"I thought you said she lived here..."

"She did. She passed away in 1948. She lived in your flat."

The elderly lady handed Janine the dust cover of the record. It was the woman she'd seen on the balcony, standing in a purple gown.

"She sang Catalan music too... with flutes. And she danced as well."

45. DEE AND ROSE

"Dee Maier", a pseudonym for a small-boned woman in her late fifties with a charming smile, lives with her best friend, "Rose", in a rural hamlet in southeastern Pennsylvania near the border to the Poconos. Miles of farmland stretch on both sides of Rose's property. Inherited from her father, who made a living as a cobbler, Rose also shared her small ranch-style home with a cat, Grace. Although the house was small, it sat on four acres of land adjacent to a farmer's soybean field and across from undeveloped land. Behind them another house sits, smaller than theirs, where their other friend, "Sally", a childless widow, lives alone.

On hot summer afternoons, Dee and Rose visit with their friend Sally and take in a matinee to get away from the oppressive heat, ordering popcorn and huge Cokes in the cooler interior of the local village movie house. They all shared a love for classical films, but Dee was also into horror films and the occasional science fiction films like *2001: A Space Odyssey*. Unlike Rose and Sally, Dee believed in the afterlife and in UFOs and abductions.

As the weather cooled in September, the two women readied

their large vegetable gardens for canning. They did a final harvest of the large plots of vegetables to make way for pumpkins, and sold the matured pumpkins in late October to the local town where Halloween was almost a religious rite. It was during one of these pumpkin harvests, when the weather turned and the sky became a darker shade of blue amid the falling leaves, that Dee had a singular encounter.

On a late Sunday afternoon in October, the sky heralded the oncoming winter with an early dusk. Wind gusts sashayed the leaves in the side yard where the farmer's field lay fallow from the first frost. Nearby, Dee placed the last of the pumpkins from the acre patch into a wood bin, ready for the hired truck to take it to town the next day. They were to follow the truck into town, as Rose was hoping to pick up some bales of hay to decorate the small front porch while Dee spoke to the farm market owner who rented them a stall. Dee was counting the edible pumpkins in another wooden bin when she felt something watching her from the farmer's field.

She looked up from her inventory, the notebook she had been scribbling on open in her hand. A flash of light behind the sole tree in the field illuminated the sheen of frost on the field. There was no one there.

She moved sideways to see what was behind the tree and saw what appeared to be a streetlight, but she determined it was too high. Then the wind blew, and to her surprise, it seemed to blow the light in her direction, away from the tree.

Now that she had a better view, it appeared to be an orb, perfectly circular like a moon, but more radiant. It didn't hurt her eyes, but it seemed to be watching her. Dee turned away, looking for Rose. She was outside alone. Dee watched as the orb began to spin and started to cross the road to the uncultivated field in front of the house.

Dee dropped the notebook and dashed for the front door,

watching from the porch. She banged on the door, calling out to Rose. The door opened, and Rose peered out. Dee pointed to the spinning orb, which was now stationary and back by the farmer's field where it had originated.

"See it? It was closer before... it's now behind the tree."

"Did you scare it?" Rose jibed.

Suddenly, the orb winked out.

"What the heck."

"A tree nymph," Rose offered. She didn't believe in UFOs like Dee did.

After dinner that night, the women settled in the living room to watch the remake of *War of the Worlds* where Tom Cruise was the star. Rose could not help put it on in light of Dee's interesting sighting. It was partly to put some levity into the evening, as Dee tended to get caught up with anomalies she had observed, as it was not the first in her life. She obsessed with trying to determine what it was, so that the topic later dominated the conversation for days.

Around 11:45 p.m., Rose had just settled into her room to retire for the night when Dee across the hallway woke up. Dee usually retired earlier than her friend, which was her custom. A distinct vibration under her pillow, which seemed to magnify, had awakened her from a dead sleep. A steady hum, like some equipment had been turned on. She sat up and looked over to her right at the window near her where the sheer curtains allowed light to enter the room. Her window faced the front porch where the road was located. She wondered whether the light had returned to the uncultivated field across the road.

She touched her headboard and felt the vibration. It was not her imagination. She needed a drink of water anyway, so she would check to see if for some reason an appliance had been left on besides the refrigerator, which was brand new. She opened her bedroom door and saw Rose's light was off underneath her door. Asleep. She turned right, then left, as the kitchen was behind Rose's bedroom.

The kitchen windows and small deck faced the back field of the house, where the vegetable rows could be viewed. One of the rows of pumpkins, the edible ones, still needed to be picked, which they saved for last, as Rose made pumpkin pies from some of them for Thanksgiving gifts and donations. Dee was lost in thought, distracted in planning the last pumpkin harvest, when she again noted the vibration. It was throughout the small house. It didn't come from the refrigerator.

As Dee poured herself a glass of cold water from the refrigerator, the field of pumpkins lit up. Something was above the house, casting a light onto the field. A ray of light, like a huge searchlight, lit up the last row. Dee backed away, observing the field. She noticed the vibration had stopped when the light came on. Quickly, Dee bolted for her cell phone, determined to take a picture of the lit pumpkins and, maybe, if she had enough courage, come out to the porch to see if she could catch a photo of the "thing" above the house.

Grabbing her cell phone, she unlocked the back door and exited onto the deck, turning her back to the railing and looking up. She caught whatever it was in time to see a darkened shadow skim the edge of the roof. The lights had once again darkened and winked out. She stepped down from the deck, ran around to the front, and saw a dark flat orb slowly "sail" away. This time it looked like a lens – a saucer. It looked to be about the size of her car.

Then, as Dee stood there shivering in her nightgown, she turned on the cell camera and flicked a photo. The flash momentarily lit up the dark orb, and it looked like a metal surface. Then it turned on its side, became small, and in a flash became the white orb she'd seen earlier. Dee ran back to the relative safety of the back deck, almost tripping on the stairs.

She shut and bolted the door and discovered Rose was standing there.

They both ran outside so Rose could see it. There was nothing. Dee looked down at her cell phone's view finder, but all she got was the field and the dark sky. Whatever it was hadn't registered.

In a few months, another strange event would occur.

46. THE ARMOIRE MIRROR AGAIN

Dee and Rose had a myriad of friends. In one of their small social gatherings at the church hall, I met up with them and showed them a photo of a haunted house where the original owner had died at an early age. As the story goes, the owner, a woman, had a favorite dresser and armoire. The woman used to primp herself in front of the armoire's mirror. The armoire – now a family heirloom, made entirely of mahogany, and fashioned in the eighteen century – sat in a spare bedroom, which had not been used for years.

I showed Dee and Rose a photo taken by my friend Mike of the armoire the year before in 2017. Mike had sent the photo as part of a collection of photos of the house they had planned to prepare to sell. I saved the photo on my smartphone. The room, now dusty with disuse, had recently been reopened so that it could be cleaned out. Mark marked the particular shot to me to point out the "anomaly" in the armoire's mirror and another "anomaly" by the window. However, I could not spot what Mark was talking about in the photo, so without biasing their perception, I shared the picture with Dee and Rose, as they had planned on antique shopping.

Mark was actually at his great-grandmother's house to visit an aging aunt who lived there alone and did not recall seeing the armoire or that particular spare bedroom despite her walk through the house. Mark and his sisters had talked about a haunted armoire, and their story was included earlier in this book. They had sighted a ghost reflected in the armoire, but for some reason thought it was a different armoire. In the photo, the armoire sat right next to a window at the time the photo was taken. The window itself was purportedly haunted.

Dee and Rose hunched together to examine the shot under the bright light of the church hall, as people mingled and socialized. Dee saw a figure of a woman in black with an unmistakable look of anger. It was a reflection in the mirror of the armoire. Rose concurred she also saw the woman. I looked at the photo again and still failed to see anything.

As Dee and Rose continued to examine the photo, Dee spotted a "helmet" sitting on the windowsill. But to her surprise, though the window was shut, the helmet appeared to be sitting outside the shut window and not inside the window as she previously thought. As it was in a smartphone, I enhanced the view to detail the window... and lo and behold, there was a helmet that looked to be like those used by Japanese soldiers. The three women shivered as I talked about World War II and the massacre in the area, which was previously mentioned in this book. I put away the cell phone and changed the topic. Soon, everyone forgot about the photo and moved on to other topics.

A month later, I came to visit Dee and Rose at their home. As we were all hikers, we frequented all the parks in the area and decided to take a quick side trip to the Twin Towers Memorial commemorating the victims who died tragically as a result of the terrorist attacks. The memorial was situated in a park about half an hour away. So off we went in Rose's car for what turned out to be a nice leisurely drive through the hills of the country-side. Shortly, we stepped out of the car at the edge of the park's car lot and walked.

As we walked through the gardens and the memorial, Dee was snapping photographs throughout. She had brought her camera along, as she had meant to go there when she heard they had shipped part of the steel rods pulled from the wreckage of the Twin Towers as part of the memorial. As Dee approached the steel frames that were burnt in the tragedy, we paused to allow her to take pictures. In one of these, Dee aimed the camera at our feet as we stood around the massive steel rod that once held up part of the building. We paused to take in the last of the garden's plants and then walked back to the car to get some dinner.

A few weeks later, Dee called and arranged to have some lunch after doing some shopping in town. The two liked shop-ping in consignment shops and thrift stores, perusing the open markets as well for antiques and clothing bargains. I sensed there was something on Dee's mind, and when we finally sat down to lunch at a local diner, Dee told me that the photographs on her camera showed one that had something that bothered her. Strangely enough, though Dee seemed anxious to impart this piece of information, she did not bring the camera nor a copy of the photo.

Apparently, in the shot, Dee saw the same "woman with an angry and malevolent look" she'd seen in the armoire etched into the 9/11 photo. Since she didn't have the camera with her, I could not see what it could be. Dee exclaimed that sometimes things attach themselves to people and that we need to pray and keep vigilant, as it takes a lot to get rid of them.

I wondered at Dee's statement, as the previous photograph I showed her was an armoire reflection miles away in a small province in the Philippines, taken by Mike, who saw it in person.

I now wondered if I would see the woman with the "malevolent look" in Dee's 9/11 photo. I was not able to see the figure in the armoire, which I thought was strange, as I tended to be sensitive to anomalous things. I had downloaded the armoire photograph in a Facebook forum for ghost sightings, and at least four other people commented and one even circled the alleged ghost in the mirror.

On a separate trip for antique and thrift store shopping, we once again met for lunch. Still waiting for the 9/11 photo from the previous visit, Dee discussed a recent hike she and Rose had done through a local park, thirty-five miles outside Philadelphia in a small town nestled in Bucks County. Once again, Dee had taken photos, this time with her smartphone, and was eager to show me a shot she'd taken of the lake.

In this photo, Dee had taken aim at the park's lake, aiming the camera down into the water as she stood at the edge. She indicated that at the time, she was just taking a shot of the water to show how clear the lake was despite its size. The lake, situated in the center of the park, was frequented by locals and visited by people in neighboring towns, who moored their small boats to fish or to do some leisure paddling around the lake. Paths meandered where people walked their dogs, and bicyclists would ride their new equipment around the challenging little paths up and down the hills around the lake.

The photo Dee proffered showed a reflection of something square and bluish above Dee, whose image was not seen in the water's reflection. Whatever the object was, it appeared to be suspended above the lake over Dee's head, but almost ahead of her, as her reflection was not included. The reflection was very pronounced so much so that one expected to see something hovering over the lake, just a mere ten meters from the viewer. But there was nothing there.

I asked Dee if there were any trees or children flying kites or drones in the area. It was highly unlikely that a drone would appear as a bluish square without any type of protrusion, as they usually appeared like a star or had arms like an octopus. Kites were more likely, where the string would not show, though it would usually appear as a triangle of sorts.

Dee said it was a weekday, and no children were around except for ones with their mothers in strollers and elderly pensioners who strolled together. I made a mental note to visit the area where they stood as soon as possible, and this time Dee emailed me the lake photo with the blue reflection.

Then Dee showed us the white mist that appeared as a cloud formation over the lake, close to the surface. Both Rose and I saw the whitish formation, but only saw what might be a cloud. Dee thought it looked like an angel. Despite examination, neither Rose nor I could make out what was apparent to Dee, except for the bluish reflection, whose structure was much more pronounced.

At the time of this writing, I had finally received Dee's photo of the 9/11 shot, which showed a shadow of a woman on the ground right next to a steel rod, which had been part of the Twin Towers. I have provided both the armoire mirror photo as well as the 9/11 shot to allow the reader to make the determination if they see anything in either or both photographs of a malevolent face.

47. THE HOUSE ON THE MOUNTAIN

In Pennsylvania, mountains are rare, but hills punctuate the landscape, especially closer to upstate New York. There is, however, a hill that is so steep that most locals call it a mountain, and it is named as such. For the purposes of this story, I will rename it "Deer Mountain", as deer are plentiful on this hill. This hill is located close to the Philadelphia area, a mere forty-five miles away.

In the pastoral landscape of this county where the mountain is located, horses, farms and undulating seas of green can be seen for miles. Homes are usually far apart and built of fieldstone; the newer developments, far and few, are usually made with brick and shingle.

A large fieldstone house, well appointed, sits nestled in the middle of the woods high up on Deer Mountain. An elderly woman in her late seventies lives there with goats, pigs and chickens. She is as vibrant and energetic as ever even in her later years.

"Alma" prefers to remain anonymous, as she lives in a remote area and loves her privacy. The nature of her encounter makes for a hair-raising story, which she shared on the anniversary of her husband's untimely death. She did not want to be alone on this day, as a year ago, when she was home and on her way to the local church in the village, she encountered something unexplained.

This story was recounted by some elderly women who worked at an animal rescue. Alma loved animals and had found a stray dog who did not get along with her chickens. After a few interludes with the chickens, Alma decided the dog was not meant for her farm. She had finally coaxed the animal with food and leash and took the dog in her truck to deliver to the vet who had a rescue. It was a timely meeting for her, as it was a day she didn't want to be alone after her encounter a year back. Having already done her chores, she wanted company and was curious about the rescue operated by her animals' veterinarian.

Upon meeting the dog, the rescue manager, who was a veterinary nurse, remarked upon the dog's huge face, as it was a pit bull, and how Alma should talk to the women about how she'd found him on the mountain. The dog was without a collar, but seemed well cared for, and its fur was clean and healthy. Perhaps someone would come looking for the dog, which seemed otherwise affectionate with humans, if a little hungry.

So Alma got an unexpected tour of the facility and met "Corrine", who remarked on her kindness and sat down with Alma for coffee after the dog was safely in a large room, being washed and fed. Corrine introduced Alma to two other elderly women who spent their retirement caring for animals that would otherwise be put down.

Comfortable with the company, Alma felt she could share with them what had happened to her on this same day a year ago, which was doubly difficult, as it was the anniversary of her husband's passing. Alma had been exhausted on that particular day, as she had picked vegetables from her garden plot, moved some hay for the goats, and changed the hay stalls in the pigsty.

She only had four goats and two pigs, but at her age, it meant an entire morning for her, plus the chickens, which laid eggs constantly.

Alma was not in the habit of going into the village for dinner, but since she was too tired to cook, she tucked herself into her small Toyota SUV and motored down the winding road that led down the "mountain". She was hoping to go to a small diner, where she could read a book she had just downloaded from Amazon, one of the few pleasures she allowed herself besides maintaining her large home and land.

As Corrine listened with her companions, Alma began her story. She had found the diner she was looking for. She also found two acquaintances who were already seated – an elderly couple who used to see movies with her and her husband. Seeing the couple made Alma feel lonelier, but she was happy when they asked her to join them, as they had just begun their own dinner. Alma ordered some seafood and became lost in the conversation. As the meal ended, they had coffee, but then the couple interrupted the conversation, as they were trying to catch a late film at the village. Would she like to join them if she was interested? It was an old Italian film. Alma took note of the time and noted it was late for her, but it was a way to spend an evening with some company. Her husband would have wanted her to go, and she had a senior citizen discount.

Alma followed the couple in her car, as the cinema was situated on the opposite corner of the village. She parked and noted it had begun to drizzle, so she quickly ran to the entrance and bought a ticket. As Alma waited for the couple in the foyer, she looked out the double doors and saw a stranger in shadow standing by himself, staring back. He seemed to have large ears protruding from his head. It gave Alma the creeps, as she had never seen anyone like him in all her trips to the village.

Alma looked away in time to see the couple enter, and she

joined them. The film was worth seeing, as it reminded her of an earlier time in her life when her husband used to travel with her to Italy. They made a note to meet again, this time planning on lunch and some shopping at an outlet.

They parted ways, and Alma walked back to her car, the rain now in earnest. She pulled out her umbrella and walked briskly, forgetting about the man across the street. She found her car and drove away towards home.

On the outskirts of the village, she noted a car with its high beams on behind her. Stupid, she thought. It made her blind to the road ahead of her, slick with water. She signaled to park and let the driver go past. As she parked, she watched the car go by and felt something watching her from the sidewalk of the quiet residential area. It was now half past ten at night. The road was punctuated by some houses in an older section of the village, close to the entrance of the highway, which she rarely took.

She moved to turn the wheel back onto the road when she saw a light flash from the sidewalk to her side. She braked and saw the same man mysteriously standing quietly, staring at her with some light on his chest. It looked like a flashlight of some kind, but his hands seemed to be at his sides, his ears very pronounced as they stuck out of his head. It made her feel frightened, as it was so sinister. The man did not move, but the light turned and aimed at her.

Alma quickly stepped on the gas pedal and reentered the small road. Quickly, she was back driving out of the village and did not look back. Ahead of her, trees parted as she edged closer to the road that joined and led to the mountain. To her right, lights in the sky seemed to be following her, shadowing her car. She looked over, distracted, and it seemed like there were three of them in a cluster.

She eased the small SUV onto the road, past the large farm on her right, the lone post office, then the right turn to the road leading to the mountain. Finally, the car began to climb, and the rain thankfully had eased off. She began to relax, anticipating the cozy house that awaited her. Though the narrow road was dark and unlit, some lights from a home or two were now ahead of her as she climbed the mountain. On a turn onto the third road, which was hers, she eased off the gas pedal, as it was the final turn, where there was a cliff nearby. This was the part of the road she dreaded driving at night, as her vision was not as good anymore. She kept the car close to the hill side so as not to take a tumble.

As the road ended, she saw the yellow mailbox to her house several yards away and aimed for it. It was now a straight path to her house. Relieved, Alma took one more look at the rearview, distracted by a light. Walking in the middle of the road with the "light" on his chest was the man!

Terrified, Alma now knew he was following her. How did he get up the mountain that fast? He was on foot. Did he leap into a car to pursue her? No, he was STILL walking. She looked at her house in the distance and gunned the motor, turning the car sharply with a screech and a tailspin. Her heart was beating fast as she tried to outdistance him. She drove into the garage, a separate structure. She attempted to calm herself, as she did not want a heart attack like the one Louie, her husband, had suffered.

As she stopped the car, she exited, now running for her back door, keys in hand. No lights so far. She got to the back terrace and turned the key, the floodlights coming on.

She slammed the door shut and turned the bolt home. As she looked around the windows of the large kitchen, she noted the animals were silent. Usually her chickens would cluck in the commotion. She quickly walked over to the front door, which faced her road, and noted the streetlamp, which marked her property, by the mailbox. She checked the bolt and waited.

Nothing. She turned and surveyed the windows in the living room and the dining room. Then a light in the hallway.

Alma walked into the hallway by the stairs. Ahead of her was the kitchen, and a light seemed to be coming from it. She knew she had not turned the light on. Slowly she walked down the hall and saw a flashlight shining through her back door. As soon as she entered the kitchen, the light turned, as if whoever was holding it had turned away. Terrified now, she approached the door and peered through. Her backyard was bracketed on one side by the garage, then the vegetable plot, then the chicken house, with the pigsty and goat barn on the far right. Did he enter the goat barn on the other side? Was he standing right by her door?

She waited. Then she saw him floating, it seemed, toward the chickens. He stopped in front of the wire door, aiming his light at the chickens. She realized that the light was emitting from the man's chest. Both his arms were at his sides.

The chickens became frantic and began a chorus of clucking, flying around the coop – a chorus of panic. They wouldn't be laying eggs tomorrow. She took a stick she usually used to close the barn windows from the top and unbolted the door, stepping out.

"Who are you?!"

Silence. Then the light on the man's chest went dark.

Unable to locate him, Alma grabbed her flashlight from the kitchen shelf and shined it on the man, whose back was to her.

"Get out! This is private property!"

The man turned away from the chickens to face her – and disappeared from sight.

Alma darted in, slammed the door, and bolted it. The man had simply disappeared. She stood at the door for what seemed like hours.

She awakened sitting on the kitchen floor, still clutching the stick. It was already 6 a.m. She must have fallen asleep.

Alma never left the house alone again to do anything late in the village. She made sure she was home by 8 p.m. and always locked all her doors. She never saw the man again, who seemed like he was very curious about her and her chickens. She never told anyone about the incident until she met the ladies at the rescue a year later.

The women gave her their phone numbers just in case she did need something at night or needed company at her house on the mountain. Especially if the man decided to return and she was alone.

48. THE SEER

Meg, which is the name this woman picked for herself, could never find the right man. She made a living in education and could not find anyone who was still single in the profession. At every school she went to (and she had transferred twice to different public schools) all the male teachers were either married or engaged, and some who were divorced were also remarried. Meg felt time was ticking, as she was already in her late thirties and wanted to have a family.

In desperation, Meg decided to meet people by joining a single professionals club. She had to go to a local diner for starters to be introduced to the rest of the members; then it became progressively more "classy", as Meg termed it, as every month went by. The last dinner took place on a ship, and the members dined on lobster bisque, some stuffed mushrooms, and a crab cake dinner. The meal was not prepared as well as Meg expected it to be, but her goal, as well as the rest of the members', was to meet someone, not to partake of culinary delights.

Meg expressed her disappointment to another woman, who

agreed with her, but seemed preoccupied with the man who was seated next to her. Finally, the man left to mingle, and the woman returned her attention to Meg. The woman was older than Meg, she guessed, by ten years and suggested she see a "psychic" who was very "good" at telling the future.

Not being religious, Meg was not averse to the idea, and as the night progressed and no one seemed to be attracted to conversing with them, they arranged a lunch date together to discuss going to the psychic – a woman who lived about an hour north in a large town by a state park.

Two weeks later, Meg joined "Sally" for lunch, and then they drove to the appointment together in Sally's new Honda. They drove north through fields, and finally at the town's marker, Meg asked her new friend how she'd met her. Sally indicated she had been brought there by another friend, a neighbor, whose sister had died in a car accident. She wanted to get in touch with her deceased sibling to find out if she was fine. According to Sally, the deceased sibling had communicated to her through the seer during the session. Had she talked to the seer since? No, Sally replied. According to the neighbor, the session had ended when the seer told the woman the sister would relay messages through dreams. And?

Sally told Meg the woman was deeply happy, as she'd had dreams of conversing with her deceased sister almost every night since then. Meg thought it was creepy, but then everyone had their own preference.

The seer lived in a small stone townhouse bordered by geraniums and ornamental grasses. Large hostas clustered around the edges of the neat home, and they entered through a small stone porch. A nondescript woman in her forties, trim and slight, ushered them in with a demure smile into the high-ceilinged, but tiny living room. The décor almost reminded Meg of a doctor's office. It was Spartan and simple. The outside looked better, in her estimation.

Sally introduced Meg to Denise, the psychic, who then examined Meg's eyes and nodded as if to understand some inner workings in Meg. Meg was a bit self-conscious, being it was her first time with a fortune-teller. She asked her if she worked with cards, and Denise replied no, only with her birth date and place of birth. Sally nodded in agreement, and they all sat around a small kitchen table. Denise repeated her fees for the sake of understanding, then asked who would like to go first.

Meg nudged Sally, who didn't care. Sally said she was ready and followed Denise into a small alcove with a door. Meg thought it was a small bathroom, but realized later it was the dining room of the small townhouse. Time passed, with Meg checking her smartphone, and then Sally came out half an hour later.

Denise motioned for Meg to enter, and she winked at Sally, who remained serious. Meg wondered how her "reading" went. They would compare notes later.

Denise began the session with Meg's birth name and her place of birth. Curiously, Denise asked Meg if she prayed routinely or had prayed before their session. Meg, who was born a Catholic, but hardly attended mass except during the Christmas holidays, replied in the negative. She didn't see a need or never thought of it. Denise counseled her to pray beforehand, as "sometimes" it was needed, depending on what the session foretold. Meg nodded, but soon forgot Denise's advice.

Denise then closed her eyes and reached for one of Meg's hands. Meg asked if she should hold both Denise's hands, but the woman said it wasn't necessary, as it was only to make contact with the recipient. Then Denise dropped Meg's hand, and she kept her eyes closed.

"They're speaking."

"Who?"

"Two men. One looks very tall with sunburnt skin, reddish blond hair, light blue eyes."

"My dad!"

"Okay. He's pointing to his watch. A big watch."

"He's always in a hurry. He likes big watches."

"The other man resembles him, but shorter with brunette hair. Younger. He said he died of cancer."

"My brother Sam."

"He is nodding his head."

"Oh."

"Your dad says you should date, but he sees your time running out."

Meg nodded knowingly and was now leaning against the chair, intrigued. "I see. What does he suggest I do?"

"Your brother says you need to be careful. He says you will meet someone soon."

"Be careful about this person I'm meeting soon?"

"Yes."

"Why? Is he not good?"

"No. They're speaking... they're now excited. They want you to be very careful. He has a bad past."

"Well, then I don't want to meet him!"

"But your dad says he is one of many. You just have to end the date if you don't feel a good vibe. He said to pray first. Your brother is nodding."

"Okay, tell them I will."

"They're talking..."

"Yes?"

"Watch your mom. Health issues with her eyes."

Meg was appalled. Her mom had cataracts and was awaiting an operation.

"Would it be good to have her cataracts removed, or is there..."

"They want you to have her go ahead with it."

"Okay."

"They said they love you and your mom."

Meg's eyes began to tear. Her father had died several years ago when she was still in college, and her brother had passed just over a year ago.

"Tell them I'm glad they're together up there."

Denise nodded. She smiled, though her eyes were closed.

"They are leaving. They are here if you need them. Just call."

"Call?"

"Call them by name."

Denise's eyes opened, and she smiled.

"Are they gone?"

"Yes. You should pray before you leave."

Meg nodded, then thanked the woman. They stood up and went back to Sally, who looked back with curiosity. Meg smiled at her friend, feeling relieved.

On the drive back to their town, Sally told Meg that Denise had indicated she would not be meeting someone soon, but would be introduced to a man she actually knew before. Sally didn't like the idea, as most men she had known before were not the type she would become serious with or go as far as marry.

Meg thought about the session and the woman's advice to be careful. She started wondering how accurate the woman was when she realized there was no way for her to know both her father and brother had passed away or how they looked. Denise had described them to a T without any information aside from Meg's full name or birthplace. She had been born in the west, so far from her hometown of Cupertino, California. There was no way Denise would know of them.

Meg entered her apartment, turned on her flat-screen TV,

which she used for background noise, and sat staring at the screen, wondering who or when she would meet this man she had to be careful about. What was the point? Was he a danger to her? She wished Denise was there to answer any more questions. Next time, she would ask, if she had the money. The woman was expensive.

49. A DATE

Meg found herself with Sally again later that month, attending a dance at a local country club. Wine and candlelight made the evening very sophisticated. Neither Meg nor Sally had ever been to the country club and knew the membership was well beyond what they could afford. Outside, a large terrace could be seen, and waiters walked around refilling drinks. The food was buffet style, but the bar, as expected, was extra.

Meg found herself sitting with a few women, including her new friend Sally. She hoped this was an evening of fun, though she didn't expect to meet anyone. At this point in her life, she was comfortable on her own and wasn't expecting to meet anyone except for other women who were also on their own. However, most of the women had children now grown and off to college or their own careers. She eventually grew tired of their conversation and decided to call it a night.

As Meg emerged onto the quiet street, she noted large homes all around the area – a neighborhood on the high end. She felt comforted somehow, feeling it was safe to walk, unlike the downtown area where her job was located. She didn't feel inclined to work overtime, as it meant walking the streets at night and onto a train platform for the way home in the suburbs of her apartment. Waiting in the bowels of the city for a train was not something she looked forward to, and she was one of the few who lived the furthest from the city.

As Meg walked toward her car, she spotted a man in the shadow of a tree, smoking. It must be another bored club member. She sensed he was one she would not care to meet, as she didn't like smokers and would not involve herself with one. She clicked her car, and the light flashed momentarily to indicate the locks were disengaged. In that momentary flash, she saw a man across the street from her car with the hood up of a shiny BMW sedan.

As Meg entered her car, she watched as the man worked on something under the hood. His face was partially obscured by the dim light and by the hood obstructing her view. As she sat in her car, deliberating whether it was a good opportunity to offer help, perhaps call someone to tow the car, the smoker approached from the shadow of the tree, and she saw what she thought was the flash of a knife, its steel blade caught in the light of the streetlamp.

She exited her car, slamming her door to indicate there was another person on the street.

Meg yelled to warn the man fixing the BMW. "Hey, can I help you?! There's people at the club we can get to help…"

Suddenly, the smoker stopped midway and looked at Meg. He backed away from the car and quickly nodded.

"Will you? I was just about to adjust the spark plugs." The man held up the penknife.

Meg shivered, wondering if it was a ruse, but the man by the BMW was now aware. He stepped away from the car and faced the smoker.

He had a young voice, though he was tall and muscular in a sports shirt and slacks.

"Thanks, but it can't be done that way. Are you from the neighborhood?"

The smoker quickly put away his knife and offered his hand to the man with the BMW.

"Jeff. I don't live here. I was a guest at that party over there." He pointed to the well-lighted country club, the music still playing inside as people milled about through the large windows.

Meg tried to relax, but was suspicious. Something about the man didn't seem right. He wasn't dressed appropriately as he should be for a country club dinner. She was wearing a dress, and the men were wearing collared shirts. Some even had sports jackets on.

The man with the BMW took the man's hand and shook it. "Jeff" walked away and told him to have a nice night. Meg felt she had averted a crime from occurring – or maybe perhaps he was really just trying to help.

"I'm Tim, by the way." (Pseudonym.)

Meg was watching the strange man leave, but then turned her attention to Tim. "Meg."

"Thanks for that. I didn't see him until he was practically on top of my car."

"I thought he had a knife."

"I saw that."

"Was he at the party with us?"

"I don't recall seeing him."

"Maybe he came out to smoke. Who knows."

"Well, he's gone. Please, let me at least buy you a cup of coffee."

Meg paused and looked at her watch. It was getting late.

"Please, it doesn't have to be tonight."

"Sorry... it's just that I have to get up early... I commute to the city..."

"I understand. Here's my card."

The man proffered his calling card. He was an undertaker.

Meg looked back at Tim and smiled a perfunctory smile.

Tim grinned back. "I know. I own it, but I don't do the embalming, just in case you were wondering."

Meg laughed and Tim laughed. That broke the ice.

"I'll take you up on that coffee."

50. THE UNDERTAKER

As luck would have it, a few weeks went by and Meg found herself at a local street market, shopping for vegetables and fruits. When she turned to get a few pastries from a vendor's stand, she made eye contact with none other than Tim. They set a date for the coming Friday to have an early dinner before the weekend. Meg felt privately that it might have been a good idea, as she didn't want to "waste" a Saturday coffee, lunch or dinner on a man who might turn out to have little in common with her or become boring. She admitted she was attracted, but it was only because he smelled of success.

The week went uneventfully and Friday came. Meg dressed in a good pair of jeans and a pretty top, but wanted to keep the date casual, like an after-hours meeting with an acquaintance, which he still was at this point. Tim offered to pick her up, and forgetting the caution counseled by the seer, Meg told him her address – a faux pas in the eyes of the dating club she'd joined. There was a safety reason for that, but Meg impulsively was taken by the idea of riding in a BMW. Meg had told Sally of the meeting in the street of the country club, and Sally had cautioned her as well. She could not give Meg any impressions of "Tim", as she had not talked to him during the networking after dinner.

Tim arrived promptly with a small bouquet, which impressed Meg as old-fashioned. She quickly let him into the apartment as she located a vase. Upon setting the flowers in a vase, she smelled them. A fleeting sense came over her that the scent seemed "heavy", but unfamiliar with the flowers, as she was not into gardening, she let it go.

The BMW coasted with ease onto the road, and soon, they were at a hilltop French restaurant, which surprised Meg. She wasn't dressed for something so upscale and indicated she would have perhaps dressed more than casually had she known. Tim grinned and told her it was a surprise, as he'd always wanted to try the restaurant, and they served as early as 5 p.m. with just a reservation the day before. He assured her it was fine, as he himself was in jeans, something he'd thrown on quickly.

It was late summer, just going into fall, so Meg agreed to sit outside on the fieldstone patio, where the waiter offered wine. Her date seemed familiar with wines and selected one for the table. Meg was impressed, but now a bit worried where the date was headed, as it was, after all, a first meeting of sorts. She thought the bouquet was fine, but the wine was clearly a vintage when the waiter returned with an entire bottle and showed them the year. It was a Grand Cru, which was expensive for a first meeting.

Tim ordered an appetizer, and Meg refused. She was determined to keep it simple and light so as to press upon him that it was just a "getting to know you" meeting. He pressed with an edge to his tone. Meg looked back with mild alarm, and Tim apologized, but then offered that he just wanted the evening to go smoothly. She reminded him of the "rules" of the dating club, and to her consternation, he laughed. "I don't believe in rules."

"What, then, do you believe in?" Meg asked.

"Spontaneity," Tim replied.

Meg relaxed, deciding to enjoy the lavish meal, letting herself go a little, then recalling the session with the seer. Well, she thought, Jeff, the man who'd accosted Tim, was the man she needed to be cautious about. This man she had inadvertently protected from being perhaps a victim of crime by being there. She reasoned she had protected him, and he was now recognizing that.

Meg enjoyed the food as Tim launched into how he grew up and, finally, how he ended up owning a mortuary. She was intrigued by his numerous degrees in business and the sciences, but chose not to enter into a PhD program, as it "stifled" his desire to begin working. He was determined not to become, as he indicated, a professional student. Meg complimented him and said it worked out in the long run. It seemed he was very successful with the business, and he remarked to Meg how his parents were proud to have an entrepreneur in the family.

Meg looked at her watch as the dinner ended, and Tim suggested they stroll and perhaps stop in at the mortuary, as he had to check on the evening schedule.

"Evening schedule?" Meg asked.

Yes, he replied, the mortuary was open until 8 p.m., and he had to check on the progress of a particular client whose deceased parent had a large viewing the following day, Saturday. Fair enough, she thought. After all, he was the CEO, even if it was a mortuary. She suggested they stop in his office first, then take a stroll, as she didn't think she wanted to end her evening with him in a funeral home.

The man complied, and shortly, the car coasted to a stop in front of a large mansion-type house, the large marquee indicating the funeral home. Meg said she'd prefer to wait for him in the car, as she didn't want to intrude, but he insisted she enter with him, as it might take some time.

Reluctantly, Meg exited the car and realized she should have driven on her own. She was impressed with the well-appointed home, more on the high end as funeral homes go, with its plush carpeting, dim lighting and, of course, comfy sofas for the grieving. Still, she felt a very brooding atmosphere, as like it or not, it was a funeral parlor.

Meg decided she didn't want to date this man further if he asked for a second date, successful or not. It was just not her comfort level to sit during a date talking about the progress of deceased people as clients. She had wondered what made him really refrain from getting a PhD. Death and taxes, the two absolutes, she mused. She guessed Tim wanted to make sure he was employed forever and never ran out of clients.

Meg went along and was introduced to a man with a rubbery complexion, who apparently handled the scheduling of things. The next man was an older gentleman, who seemed to have a sense of humor, though macabre, joking about the choice of "attire" of the deceased. It was poor form, but Meg laughed along as Tim proceeded to check on how things were going with the two employees. He then asked her if she'd like to take a tour, and Meg politely declined. However, Tim once again got an edge to his tone, and Meg wished she had driven her own car, as it seemed an opportune time to exit.

Meg ventured that she needed to use the powder room.

"Let's just quickly go to my office. There's a private toilet there."

Meg followed, taking note of the vases, which appeared to be antiques, but much too ornate for her tastes. She hoped his house was not as ostentatious, but she caught herself, knowing she didn't want to date him further.

Tim entered a large office paneled in some type of oak, where a large wooden desk in high polish sat in the middle. It looked more like a lawyer's office than an undertaker's. He must have come from money, she mused.

He pointed to an unmarked door set in one side of the room, and she turned the latch and entered. The bathroom was tiled tastefully in an Italian Renaissance décor. She marveled at the washbasin, which was all glass.

Meg exited and found herself in an embrace.

She pushed him away, momentarily surprised.

Tim reached again, this time attempting a kiss. She kissed him on the cheek instead and said the night was getting late and thanked him for the dinner.

He laughed.

He had a wine bottle nearby, to her surprise, obviously taken out of the refrigerator very recently. He had it on a bed of ice nearby.

He reached for it.

"Before you go? How about a glass or two? This is white."

"No, I prefer not to. I brought home paperwork. I really need to be going."

Despite her request, she sensed Tim was not ready to end the evening. He reached for her hand, kissing it. Meg blushed with the chaste gesture, thinking it was opposite to his forward behavior just minutes before.

"I really appreciate the dinner..." Meg never finished her sentence.

Tim kept her hand in a grip and, with the other, placed the cold bottle of wine against her arm.

Meg jumped away with the cold. She attempted to wipe her arm with her hand.

"What?"

Tim laughed. "I like my women cold." He approached, placing the bottle against her lips. Meg backed away again, now very concerned.

"You must be joking!"

He shook his head. "Come into the next room."

"I... I don't think so." Meg turned and opened the door.

"I'm just playing with you, Meg."

"You're spooking me."

Tim laughed. "Have you ever been to a funeral parlor before?"

"No, and I don't think I want to spend more time here than necessary."

"Please. Just one kiss. The door is open, and my men are out there."

Tim approached, then suddenly pressed the cold bottle on her lips.

Meg dashed out of the room and past the foyer, exiting the door.

Outside, disoriented, Meg watched for signs on the road. She saw she was near the train station.

Briskly, she walked, ignoring Tim's yells from the open door. Eventually, his voice faded, and Meg found herself running, reaching for her smartphone as she walked across the parking lot of the train station. Thankfully, at that late hour she just caught the 9:10 train.

She stepped in as the train's doors pulled shut.

AFTERWORD

The first half of this book chronicles a segment of one woman and her family's life from the early '60s to the 1990s. The experiences drew from the multiple tragedies of mayhem and destruction resulting from World War II casualties. Some resulted in demonic manifestations, from a nun in a black habit who leaves a mark on a child's thigh, to a shadow being who is seen smoking a cigarette outside a child's window after a mothman-like apparition heralds the suicide of a parent.

The second half chronicled a myriad of encounters from several people from all over the globe: Bigfoot, elementals who live in mounds, a full-size praying mantis, a "Tiyanak", to bedroom visitors from the sky resulting in (or helping to diagnose) cancer, and unexplained creatures at a French farmhouse. Then there are the ghosts at a haunted university, a burial ground that won't stay covered, a signing ghost, a creature that lives in a tree, and a man (or is he?) whose tendencies in amorous relationships border on the dead instead of the living.

What do all these encounters have in common? The encounters come from all walks of life, all ages and all religions. Not one person was mentally imbalanced when they were interviewed, and subsequent conversation by phone or in person yielded years later the same account. Most had more to lose than to gain by sharing the information they gave in the formulation of this book. One in particular was a reputable professional within a small community, who would lose their career if identified.

Scientists who practice "hard" science usually look at such accounts as manifestations of dreams, perhaps a predisposition to confabulate (to make up stories for secondary gain or profit) or just a tendency to engage in wild imaginings. Some, like John Mack, a highly respected psychiatrist, and Dolores Cannon, a highly esteemed hypnotherapist, believe that these encounters are proof of existences that remain hidden from our 3D world and have been so through the beginning of time.

What remains fascinating to me as an author of these books into the realm of the fantastic is how the person who had these experiences is never quite the same. They have gained a worldview that is no longer limited to the palpable. Their perspectives have readied them to entertain what could only be seen before as science fiction. Some have become more receptive to our possible reasons for living, our place in the cosmos, and the possibility of other realities that exist side by side. Some now know that there are forces beyond ourselves who control creation and some that are so ancient that the knowledge we consider new is truly a millennium old or even older.

In some cases, people who are open to these experiences by virtue of past experiences appear to be people who had previous histories of such encounters. For some, it appears generational, as in the first half of the book, where some members of the family have had encounters prior to the haunted neighborhood where Lisa lived and grew up. Her grandmother both had ghostly encounters and a close encounter of a second kind: In the same house.

Then there are some where it appears that their steadfast and hard-nosed view of reality was shaken by an encounter that forever changed them from a conservative individual who only believed in three dimensions, to one who now engages in meditation to produce altered states of consciousness. Some are now reading books like the one the reader is reading now.

For those whose realities were tested and broadened, defied by what could only be seen in certain circles as a "miracle", the encounter itself has become a catalyst for change.

That has made it all worth it.

Postscript

At the time of the writing of this conclusion, which I penned exclusively for the second edition, my thoughts have turned to the concept of thoughtforms, or "Tulpas", as the Tibetan Buddhists call these creations. Unlike other manifestations where the energy comes from another being such as an apparition or ghost, an alien visitor or a cryptid, the "Tulpa" does not have a sentient soul. It is a creation driven from the energetic quality of human thought. The concept of a thoughtform was examined and studied extensively by Alexandra David-Neel, an anthropologist who studied mystical concepts under the tutelage of the lamas of Tibet for fourteen years. David-Neel, a Frenchwoman, lived at the turn of the century and published two books, *My Journey to Lhasa* and the subsequent book *Magic and Mystery in Tibet*, which was first published in French in 1929. David-Neel examined the concept of how human thought was powerful enough to create a physical manifestation over a period of time. A being without spirit, pressed into existence by force of will and emotion.

It is the topic of thoughtforms, or "Tulpas", that will be the second part of this volume, among more accounts and stories.

It is my intention to share with you the world of the thought-form and stories that will transcend you: People whose imagination and emotion together created a being that can be seen and felt.

To keep in touch with the author on the progress of
"Portal: The Slender Man and Other Beings",
follow Anna Maria Manalo on Facebook
or on Twitter: @FoxNRosanna
To contribute stories for consideration:
Cinescriber@gmail.com
Thank you for reading my book.

ABOUT THE AUTHOR

Anna Maria Manalo was born and raised in a suburb of Manila, where her neighborhood was replete with encounters with beings from another dimension. As a small child, she came to know and experience hauntings and uncanny events that her neighbors and family members had encountered.

Anna has been a guest on *Coast to Coast* with Connie Willis, *Midnight in the Desert* with Dave Schrader, *The Outer Limits Show* with Chris Evers, as a guest with Lon Strickler on *Arcane Radio,* Gene Steinberg's *The Paracast*, with Howard Hughes on UK radio, *Night Dreams Talk Radio* with Gary Anderson, with host David Young of *Paranormal Dimensions*, with Mike Vara of *Late Night in the Midlands*, and with Tim Beckley in *Exploring the Bizarre*.

Anna starred as Elisa Simon on episode two of the television pilot, *UFOs Over Earth* in "The Bucks County Flap" as herself while a UFO investigator for MUFON. Some of the most prominent cases she investigated are part of this book.

A screenwriter with numerous accolades earned from competitions in the US, Anna is also an artist and travel photographer. She has traveled to over twenty-six countries, encountering tourists and locals who had the most riveting accounts. She lives with her husband and a labradoodle and a goldendoodle in Pennsylvania.

～

Stories for compilation in her next volume are welcome.

To submit stories for consideration:
On Facebook: Anna Maria Manalo
On Twitter: @FoxNRosanna
Or by email at:
Cinescriber@gmail.com

Made in the USA
Las Vegas, NV
26 February 2023

68144860R00194